DIGGING TO WONDERLAND

Grandparents I never knew: Marguerite and
Harlen Gerlach, Sierra Madre, California, 1930

DIGGING TO WONDERLAND

*

MEMORY PIECES

*

DAVID TRINIDAD

TURTLE POINT PRESS

BROOKLYN, NEW YORK

Requests for permission to make copies of any part of the work should be sent to:
Turtle Point Press, 208 Java Street, 5th Floor, Brooklyn, NY 11222
info@turtlepointpress.com

Library of Congress Cataloging-in-Publication Data
Names: Trinidad, David, 1953- author.
Title: Digging to Wonderland : memory pieces / David Trinidad.
Description: First edition. | Brooklyn, NY : Turtle Point Press, [2022] |
Identifiers: LCCN 2021039325 | ISBN 9781933527284 (paperback)
Subjects: LCSH: Trinidad, David, 1953- | Trinidad, David, 1953-—Childhood and
youth. | Gay teenagers—United States--Biography. | Young gay men—United States—
Biography. | Poets, American—Anecdotes. | California, Southern—Biography.
Classification: LCC PS3570.R53 Z46 2022 | DDC 811/.54
[B]—dc23/eng/20211117
LC record available at https://lccn.loc.gov/2021039325

Some of the pieces included here were previously published in
the following journals: *Air/Light, The American Poetry Review,
BlazeVOX, Cherry Tree, Columbia Poetry Review, Elderly,
Hair Trigger, Indiana Review, The Iowa Review, Peripheries,
Plume, Southern Florida Poetry Journal, The Yale Review*.

Design by Crisis
Cover photograph: David Trinidad,
high school yearbook photo, 1971.

ISBN 978-1-933527-28-4

First Edition

Printed in the United States of America

FOR EULA AND JOHN

With all the lost details, you could have made a new world.
—Pierre Reverdy

CONTENTS

DIGGING TO WONDERLAND

KEVIN FROM HEAVEN

was a one-man moving service. He drove a little white truck (about the size of a milk truck) and quickly moved your possessions from one address to another. I don't remember who told me about him. He got most of his business word of mouth. In 1990, he moved me from a sublet on the Lower East Side to a sublet in the West Village, then, not long after that, from the West Village to SoHo. A graduate student, I didn't have many possessions, mostly boxes of books and a fold-out futon. Maybe a side table or two, a few lamps. Kevin was stocky, with a full head of curly brown hair. He was friendly, and moved you fast, stuffing everything into his little white truck. (Come to think of it, his truck may have been a converted milk truck.) He wore a wide leather weightlifting belt. I watched him hoist my folded-up futon frame on his back and carry it down five flights of my 2nd Street walk-up. I was amazed. And a little worried for him. When his truck was loaded, I would go with him in the passenger seat. He drove as fast as he moved objects; I bounced with each bump. He encouraged me to tell others about him, and I did. He ended up moving many of my friends. "Kevin from Heaven!" we'd all light up, whenever anyone mentioned his name.

MY PEA COAT

Laureen, a friend from my high school drama class, called and said she'd read that Western Costume, the company that supplied costumes to the movie studios, was selling off a large part of their inventory. Did I want to go? My mother gave me permission, and ten dollars. What kind of costume could I buy with only ten dollars? That Saturday morning, we drove to Hollywood. 1970: the air still relatively crisp, the sky still relatively blue. Laureen let me smoke in her car. Driving anywhere outside of the Valley was an adventure—a glimpse of the still relatively scary real world. We parked on Melrose Avenue, down the street from Paramount Pictures, and walked to the monolithic costume warehouse. Once inside, we encountered row after row of floor-to-ceiling clothing. Laureen found several items, including a theatrical fur-trimmed stole that she ever after referred to as her "countess wrap." I don't know what drew me to the pea coat. I pulled it from a rack of densely packed jackets. A heavy wool, double-breasted, navy blue coat with anchors on its six plastic buttons. It fit just right, and cost ten dollars. I loved my pea coat, wore it everywhere. I can see myself trudging to high school on a chilly morning, light fog drifting over clipped suburban hedges, furtively lighting a cigarette then slipping my pack of Marlboro 100's back into one of its slit pockets. In time the inside lining split, my pea coat began to fall apart. Undoubtedly it ended up in a bag destined for the Goodwill.

Decades later I have to ask: How many extras are wearing my pea coat in old war movies? Aren't all of our clothes costumes? Was I a sailor in a past life?

3373 Overland Avenue, #2. Dennis' address. First floor, second apartment on the left. The curtain, through which he'd look out to see who had knocked, was sagging, partly detached. Inside: a sense of controlled mess. A card table was Little Caesar Press: envelopes, address lists, stacks of books and manuscripts. Evidence of copious correspondence. His lifeline to the greater world. A large framed black-and-white Hockney drawing: Gregory doing something or other. Shelves with his collections of books and albums, neatly alphabetized. A turntable on which he'd play songs for me. Such as "Mickey Mouse" from Sparks' latest, *Angst in My Pants*. Dennis loved Disneyland. And Sparks. A group of us—Dennis, Amy, Jack, Bob and Sheree, Ed—went to see them at the Whisky a Go Go. At the door, each of us was handed a "Sparks Moustache." A black Hitleresque fake mustache, in a tiny plastic bag. Everyone put them on when Sparks sang "Moustache." But I kept mine unopened—memento of a night out with "the gang."

Dennis and I spent a lot of time together in those days. We'd meet at Overland, hang out for a while, then, in his car, make the rounds: Beyond Baroque (to check up on things), Papa Bach's (where we'd scour the chapbooks and little magazines in the poetry section, a square enclosure in the back of the store), La Cabaña on Rose Avenue (where a woman stood making tortillas at a brick oven in the center of the restaurant), Tower Records on Sunset. We both chain-smoked as we talked about poems and songs, upcoming readings, New York, fame. Inevitably we'd drive down Santa Monica Boulevard, so Dennis could check out the hustlers. Circling, if one was suitably young, the block several times. We often spotted John Rechy: leather jacket and jeans, leaning seductively against a building, too old for his pose. A relic from his *City of Night*, that furtive world where all was seedy, dangerous, dim. Dennis was appalled. Rechy was the past, old hat. The future of literature (and sex) was ours.

Back on Overland, there were always unwashed dishes in the kitchen sink. My hands smelled like mildew after I used the bathroom towel.

CONFESSION

It's something I'm not supposed to say, so I'll say it: I have some of Sylvia Plath's hair. In 2009, when I was doing research in the Plath archive at the Lilly Library at Indiana University, I met K., a local scholar. We became friendly. K. had been doing Plath research for many years. An abundance of Plath hair is cataloged in the archive: locks of baby hair, teenage ponytails, tresses, amber braids. Plath's mother saved everything. One night at dinner I confessed to K. that I'd been tempted to steal a few strands of Plath's baby hair, but decided against it. Just the thought made my hands shake. K. freely admitted that, in the days before the library had security cameras, she stole some of it. "I'll give you some." "*Really?*" "I have to find it first. It's in the house somewhere." After I returned home, I emailed K. and reminded her of her offer. She wrote that she'd let me know when she located it. Months went by. I reminded again. "Still haven't found it," she replied. I began to doubt that she would come through. But eventually she did, and sent me, in an envelope on which she'd written "baby hair," much more than I expected: a small golden-brown mass. K. also sent some to P., a fellow Plathoholic. (When I confessed to P., he divulged that he too was a recipient of K.'s contraband.) I told J., a poet friend and Plath fan, about my secret stash. With tweezers, I carefully extracted a couple of strands from the mass and, the next time I saw J., presented them to her. J. later told me she inserted them (with tweezers, no doubt) into an empty pill capsule (think: *The Bell Jar*), which she placed in her red Sylvia Plath matchbox, alongside a tiny white plastic horse (think: "Ariel") and silver charms of a typewriter and half-moon. J. had pasted the matchbox with pictures of a bee, Plath, a woman's hand listlessly holding a glued-on miniature red silk rose, and a quote from one of Plath's poems: *the coffin of a midget.*

For a while I misplaced the baby hair. It was in the house somewhere, but for the life of me I couldn't find it. At last I came across it: I'd put it in a box of photographs for safekeeping. When I first received the baby hair from K., I bought, on Amazon, a small red wooden box to put it in. Made in Poland. Decorated with hearts and flowers. Plathian: *I have painted little hearts on everything.* But it remains in K.'s envelope. I've yet to give the hair a proper home.

Up till all hours lost on the Internet. Watching clips of old movies on YouTube. Clicking through a bottomless rabbit hole of Wikipedia hyperlinks. Here's what I learned about Una Merkel. American stage, film, radio, and television actress. Born December 10, 1903, died January 2, 1986. Likeable, wisecracking best friend, in innumerable movies, of stars like Jean Harlow, Ginger Rogers, Carole Lombard, Loretta Young. Best known (possibly) for her saloon brawl with Marlene Dietrich in *Destry Rides Again* (1939). Many may remember her as the housekeeper in *The Parent Trap*—the original 1961 version—one of her final roles. On March 5, 1945, Merkel was almost killed when her mother, Bessie, with whom she was sharing an apartment in New York City, committed suicide by gassing herself. Merkel was overcome by the five jets her mother had turned on in their kitchen and was found unconscious in her bedroom. Merkel herself attempted suicide nearly seven years to the day that her mother died, on March 4, 1952, by overdosing on sleeping pills. She survived, and lived another thirty-four years, dying at the unobjectionable age of 82. In one of her last interviews, she said, "I don't remember in all those years ever being with unpleasant people." Lucky girl. So what unhappiness led her to attempt an early exit? Married to an aviation executive in her thirties, divorced after World War II. No children. And I learned this about the casting of *Lost Horizon*: Director Frank Capra originally wanted 56-year-old retired stage actor A. E. Hanson for the High Lama, felt Hanson was just right for the part. Capra made a call to the actor's home, and the housekeeper who answered the phone was told to relay the message to Hanson that the part was his. Not long after, the housekeeper called back to inform Capra that when Hanson heard the news, he had a heart attack and died on the spot. Evidence of cruel fate or simply exiting on a high note, a fortuitous opportunity? There's no hyperlink for A. E. Hanson, and very little information about him on the Internet. His art a temporal link to a live audience. How I love old movies. Silvery and obsolete as the moon. Full of indispensable humanity. Jean Arthur, luminous comedienne (I've been watching a lot of screwball comedies this summer), one of the highest-paid actresses of the 1930s, reclusive as Garbo later in life. Arthur was arrested and jailed in 1973 for trespassing on a neighbor's property to console a dog she felt was being mistreated. An animal lover her entire life, Arthur said she trusted them more than people. At her trial, before she took the stand, her lawyer advised her to play it like a scene out of a Frank Capra movie. "I love the dog," she testified, "and the dog loves me." Faintly Capraesque. Unmoved, the judge fined the former star $75.00, and placed her on three years' probation.

JULY 28, 2016

ON VACATION FROM THE DEATH CAMP

How does one spend such a vacation? Ernst Bauch, an SS-*Unterschar-führer* (junior squad leader), committed suicide in December 1942 in Berlin while on vacation from his duties at Sobibor. He was thirty-one years old. Did guilt pull the trigger? bite the cyanide pill? Actually, suicide seems like the perfect way for a Nazi to spend a vacation from a death camp. Would that they all had followed suit. Another Nazi (who lived to a ripe old age, albeit in prison) said that at night they didn't talk about what they did during the day (i.e., kill thousands of people). They just drank and played cards. The banality of evil, indeed.

It is August. I am on vacation (from teaching). While I've still got free time, would someone please make this obsession with the Holocaust stop.

GUARDIAN ANGELS

You probably won't believe this. In the mid-1980s, I dated, briefly, a young man named Steve, who was HIV positive. I lived in Los Feliz; he, in Pasadena. A half-hour's drive in light traffic. Much of our time together was spent deliberating about safe sex. Condoms of course—no question— for penetration, if we ever got that far. Kissing and sucking cock OK, though were they really risk-free? We'd hold each other's hands as we talked, kiss each other's necks. But what about sweat? Wasn't it a bodily fluid. Finally, I'd had enough. One day, after I'd driven home from work, parked in my garage, and gone upstairs to my apartment, I decided I was going to drive to Steve's and have full-on sex with him. Do whatever we wanted. Precaution be damned. I went down to the garage, got in my car. Which wouldn't start. I tried and tried. You'll probably think that I flooded the engine. But I don't believe I did. I waited, then tried again. It just wouldn't turn over. I went back to my apartment, defeated and frustrated. Steve, half an hour away, was unaware. The next morning before work, I went down to my car and turned the key in the ignition. It started right up.

POLITICS AND THE NEWS

Womanspace. Los Angeles. January 31, 1973. The gallery was packed. Most of us sat on the floor. Mostly women (this was, after all, their space). Many afros, ponchos, denim work shirts embroidered with peace signs and flowers. Feminist artist Judy Chicago introduced the speaker, Anaïs Nin, with a reverent anecdote. When she arrived for brunch at Nin's Silverlake residence, Nin was in her kitchen making fresh orange juice for her guest. Chicago watched with disbelief: How could the hands that wrote the famous diary, so delicate and refined, do anything as ordinary as squeeze oranges. The audience laughed warmly and welcomed her with thunderous applause. Elegant in a black dress, hair braided into a crown, Nin read passages from her diary about Henry Miller, Otto Rank, Antonin Artaud, and her father. Then engaged with the audience. After she'd answered a few questions, a butch woman stood up and tried to take Nin to task. *Everything you read was about men. Why haven't you written about women?* A murmur of assent quickly passed through the crowd and erupted into angry chatter. Judy Chicago leapt to Nin's defense. *Anaïs has written about many women, most importantly herself. Read the diary.*

When the commotion quieted down, a young man with shoulder-length hair raised his hand. Nin called on him. He was an artist, he said, but every morning after reading the newspaper, he was so depressed by what was happening in the world he found it impossible to paint. Not one to dwell on the world's ills, and supremely practical, Anaïs simply suggested he paint first, and read the newspaper afterward.

REMNANT

Sue, whom I met in high school, in Mr. Carrelli's drama class, had long frizzy red hair and seemed wiser than her seventeen years. She'd suffered: lost her mother young, to cancer. Her dead mother collected early American antiques. I learned this the one time I went to her house, to rehearse. Spinning wheel, wooden butter churn, Windsor chairs. Sue and her younger sister Andie resented their stepmother, a blonde shiksa nurse whom their Jewish doctor father had married too soon after their mother died. That one time I was at her house, Sue made a snide remark. (I don't remember about what.) "How can you say that?" I said. "It's easy," she replied. "I just move my lips and the words come out of my mouth." I remember seeing Kurt Vonnegut's *Slaughterhouse-Five* laying open on Andie's bed. Sue drove a red VW van. (I envied classmates who had cars.) I acted with her and her boyfriend Scott in a scene from *Hamlet* in a regional Shakespeare competition. Scott played Hamlet, Sue played Gertrude, and I played Polonius. I hid behind imaginary curtains and Scott stabbed me with an imaginary sword. I fell to my imaginary death. We didn't advance to the second round. One night a group of us smoked grass in Sue's van and then scaled the fence of a closed park and wandered around in the dark. One of the first times I was high. It was a windy night. It all felt very daring and exciting. In our senior year, Sue had the lead part of Annie Sullivan in *The Miracle Worker*. I was cast as the doctor, a

14

bit part at the beginning of the play. I got to say the first line: "She'll live." My black hair was sponged with white makeup to make it look gray. Mr. Carrelli made me leave it on for the entire play, even though my part was over, for the curtain call. I sat backstage and did homework, old before my time. (Now my hair is gray for real.) After graduation, all my friends from drama class went off to college. They were going into the world to live their lives, while I was stuck at home. (My father refused to pay for anything but a local school.) Sue attended a university in Israel. She wasn't the kind of person who looked back. The last I heard (decades ago), she was still in Israel. She'd become an Orthodox Jew, married a rabbi, had twins.

That's it. A remnant. A little piece of the mosaic. A few details about someone I knew in my adolescence. Who went on to live her life, just as I've lived mine.

PROUSTIAN

My eighth-floor office at school, shortly before a night class. I need a pick-me-up, so I take the elevator down to Michigan Avenue and, at the Starbucks next door, order a medium (I refuse to say "grande") Earl Grey tea. Thinking I might need more than caffeine to get through class, I buy a little 3-pack of madeleines. Which I end up not eating (I'm trying to lose weight). After class I leave them in Lisa Fishman's mailbox with a Post-it note: "Dip in tea for that Proustian moment." When Lisa later thanks me, she says she shared the madeleines with her son, James, and her husband, Henry. Rather than summoning up their own childhood memories, they each, as they tasted the tea-soaked cookies, remembered something about *me*. James remembered that when he was younger, I gave him two pieces of furniture for the dollhouse they found on the street: a sparkly blue salon drum chair and a silky pink boudoir chaise longue (vintage Petite Princess "fantasy furniture" I won on eBay). Lisa put this in one of her poems in *Current*. She remembered that when James first met me at a poetry reading, he mysteriously asked, "Do you have a boy?" And Henry remembered picturing me reading *Valley of the Dolls* while watering apple trees in the orchard my parents bought in the Sierra Foothills in the San Joaquin Valley and hauled us to every weekend. I need no madeleine to remember those torturous weekends of my teenagehood. Instead of going to movies or parties with friends, I got to

16

irrigate the orchard, moving the hose (water was being pumped from a pond down below), a folding chair, and a hoe (in case I encountered a rattlesnake) from tree to tree. In the time it took to fill each basin, I managed to read a few pages of whatever book I had with me. It wouldn't have been *Valley of the Dolls*, sadly (that tale of sex and drugs was verboten). More likely some romantic mystery by Mary Stewart or historical family saga by Taylor Caldwell. Sherry, a pretty girl from my high school drama class, who was a regular on *American Bandstand*, once invited me to be her dance partner on the show. My father wouldn't allow it. They filmed on Saturdays, and I had to go to the apple orchard. That weekend was particularly painful. Rather than watching out for rattlesnakes, I could have been dancing on TV.

THE MOVIE OF HER LIFE

FOR PETER K. STEINBERG

One of the joys of Sylvia Plath research is how deep you can delve into her experience. There's such an abundance of material (Plath was an amazing self-documenter), one could spend years (I have) sifting through her writing and archives, obsessively investigating, following leads, putting the pieces together, and hardly make a dent. It's like you're watching the movie of her life, and that movie keeps getting bigger and bigger the longer you look at it. Focus on a day, a week, a month, any period of her life, and documentation begins to amass around it—letters, journal entries, poems, short stories, calendars, photographs, memorabilia—creating an almost three-dimensional portrait, a hologram of the poet in real time.

Take, for instance, the weekend of May 11, 12, and 13, 1951. Plath, an eighteen-year-old freshman at Smith College, traipses off for a weekend at Yale, where her boyfriend, Richard (Dick) Norton (the prototype for the character of Buddy Willard in *The Bell Jar*), is in his senior year. Plath chronicles the weekend in a May 14 letter to her mother, Aurelia Plath. Friday afternoon, Plath gets a lift to New Haven from her classmate Marcia Brown, who is driving home to New Jersey for the weekend.

Dick meets her at Union Station and they dine at Jonathan Edwards, Dick's residential college at Yale. They attend a performance of Thornton Wilder's *The Skin of Our Teeth* across the street at Yale University Theater. (Plath taped the program in her scrapbook; I didn't recognize the names of any of the actors in the production, all members of the Yale Dramatic Association—none, apparently, went on to fame—but learned the curtain went up at 8:00 p.m.) The next night, Dick wrote a letter to Aurelia, whom he called "aunt" (the families lived near each other in Wellesley, Massachusetts), also recounting the events of that weekend. He reports that seeing the play was her daughter's idea ("she took us") and that they enjoyed "the obvious but delightful symbolism about the perils and persistence of the human race." In her letter, Plath describes the play as "delightful – loud and obvious, but fun."

Saturday morning, they consume a large breakfast (per Dick). Before noon, Plath "had taken us" (he appears to be the passive type) on a "tour of bookshops, libraries, and classes." Plath sits in on (she tells this) Dick's Contemporary Events class; she finds the instructor stimulating. They then browse a bookstore. Dick buys a physics text for forty-nine cents, "for summer scientific review." By noon (says Dick) Plath is hungry enough to eat "a college-size lunch of tuna fish salad." Plath informs Aurelia that they bought their lunch at Jonathan Edwards and picnicked "on a hotel overlooking my dear blue ocean." From what she noted on her calendar, I determined that this was at Sachem's Head, a rock-walled harbor in the town of Guilford, twenty miles east of New Haven. The two play volleyball all afternoon, inhale beers and hotdogs, then sit on the stony shore reading Hemingway out loud. This Dick depicts as "solid bliss": "The sun shone, and the sea roared and splashed." There they were, "an unhurried pair of young humans in old trousers and woollen sweaters" reading Hemingway, talking, or "simply taking account of the unending sea." If it weren't for his letter, we wouldn't know that they read from Hemingway's short stories, rather than one of his novels. After bliss, hamburgers are in order. They head back to New Haven. In Dick's room, he writes his letter to Aurelia while "Syl" reads a book by his side. (What book she reads is a mystery.) Before turning in, they have milkshakes with Dick's younger brother Perry (also enrolled at Yale), who, in Sylvia's eyes, is "as lovable as ever."

For Plath, Sunday was "*the* best." After breakfast with Perry (it's disappointing when we're *not* told what they eat), Dick and Sylvia change into "dungarees" (fifties-speak for blue jeans) and sweaters (the same outfits from the day before?) and hop on a bus to Lighthouse Point (a distance of 6.3 miles, according to Google Maps) for a day of sun and sand. Hardly anyone is around. Plath collects shells, smells the pungent seaweed and mudflats, as Dick pitches stones out so far the wind catches and lifts them "in twisted eddies of air." They run on the beach, lie on the warm rocks, looking up at the blue sky and talking, and dozing on and off. Plath's face turns red-brown; Dick's, "his characteristic shade of pink." At 4:30, they return to New Haven for "a huge gourmetish meal": shrimp cocktail, minestrone soup, lamb chops, and potatoes. For dessert: milk and apple pie. "Best weekend yet," Plath wrote in her scrapbook, on the program of *The Skin of Our Teeth*, "all with the enchanting Dick ..."

In letters to Marcia Brown, Plath relates the story of Dick's graduation present. Three weeks after their Yale idyll, Plath (at Aurelia's suggestion) goes to the shopping district in downtown Wellesley and buys him an LP of César Franck's *Symphony in D Minor*. She seems to resent doling out cash for this. To make up for her sacrifice, she buys herself eight books, among them Hemingway's *The Sun Also Rises* and Faulkner's *Sanctuary* (Plath's copies are held by Lilly Library; you could go to Indiana and study her annotations). She gives Dick his gift that Saturday night (June 9), at the Norton residence (47 Cypress Road), where they are babysitting Dick's seven-year-old brother, David. After tucking David in bed, Sylvia and Dick sit in the living room and listen to Franck's symphony. Sixty-six years, eleven months, and four days later, I sit at my computer in Chicago and listen to it with them (on YouTube).

PINK AND BLACK

Everyone should have, hidden in their closet, a present that they've never opened. A gift just sitting there in the dark, like an unshared secret. I've got one in mine. I bought it eight or nine years ago when I was at an academic conference in Washington, D.C. For several stressful days, I sat in a hotel suite interviewing candidates for a position at our college. I'd never been on a hiring committee before; I over-empathized with the nervous candidates. One day after lunch, I had a little time before the next interview. In no hurry to return to the stifling atmosphere of that suite, I ducked into one of the stores off the hotel lobby (Thomas Pink), thinking I might buy myself a new shirt. Instead, I was attracted to a scarf: black, cashmere, with two thin pink stripes at either end. It was expensive, but I had to have it. And I deserved it—for sitting through those grueling interviews. "Is this a gift?" the salesman asked. I automatically answered yes. A secret gift to myself. He folded tissue over it and lowered the lid of the pink-and-black Pink box, which he tied with black ribbon (into a bow). To the ribbon he secured a little Pink gift card (blank to this day). He then, with scissors, cut V-shapes into the ribbon ends. Then slipped the box into a pink-and-black Pink bag. When I got home, I didn't have the heart to open it. It was so flawlessly wrapped. I'll open it later, I told myself. Every now and then, when I come across it in my closet, I think: Should I open it now? But I never do. Will I ever? Shouldn't everyone die with a secret in their closet? Of course it's no longer a secret now that I've written this.

DRUNK DREAM

Izzy invited me to contribute to an anthology on drinking dreams, and I was going to write to her and say, I don't really have drunk dreams anymore, in thirty-five years of sobriety I've only had a handful that I can remember, mostly when I was new, and then just sporadically over the years, but before I could write to her, I had a drunk dream, triggered no doubt by her email, I was standing at a party with a woman, a celebrity, her dress sparkled with tiny amber beads, the wall behind us yellow, light from a lamp cast a golden glow, then looking down at the glass of white wine in my hand, that sudden dread and panic, what am I doing drinking, how could I have thrown my sobriety away, all that time, the gift that's made it possible to live a long and productive life, gone in an instant, and then waking with intense relief, it isn't real, oh thank god, I'm lying here in bed in the dark, it was only a dream.

HIDDEN

In the weeks before Christmas, I'd sneak around the house when my mother was out shopping or (riskier) preoccupied in the kitchen, searching for hidden presents. Silently I'd open closet doors, slide dresser drawers, careful not to disturb the stacks of perfectly folded towels, the piles of neatly arranged clothes. Crouching down, I lifted the ruffled bedskirt and peeked under the bed in the master bedroom. There was my father's rifle, safely zipped in its long brown leather case. Many of the presents I discovered were already wrapped (in paper with Santas and snowmen and candles and candy canes); I could only guess at what was inside, and who they were for. In the hamper in the back bathroom, I found, in a Sears shopping bag, *Combat!*, the board game based on the World War II TV show. Rugged Vic Morrow, wearing an army helmet and firing a submachine gun, was on the cover; behind him: tanks, explosions, rubble. This gift, I was sure, was for my older brother. He and my father (not I) watched the show. In my excitement at having found it, I couldn't contain myself. I had to tell my mother. Like with other things, I would be in her confidence. It was a secret the two of us would share—until Christmas morning. I would even offer to wrap it for her. But anger flared, in front of the sink in the pink kitchen. My mother, who was always loving (though often harried), turned and slapped me across the face.

IN THE LATE FIFTIES,

on a Saturday afternoon, we drove in our yellow-and-white station wagon from the Valley to downtown Los Angeles so my father could buy hops for the beer he had decided to brew on his own, as an experiment, in the small, windowless laundry room he also used as a darkroom, photography being one of his hobbies. In the back seat, I looked out the window. Compared to the suburbs, the city was a foreboding place. Nothing but concrete. And such big, impersonal buildings. We stopped at a traffic light. A man was asleep on a bus stop bench. I pointed this out to my parents. Did they explain that this was skid row? That the man was either destitute or drunk, or both? His clothes shabby, his white hair disheveled, a pair of round glasses on his face. While we were still stopped, I watched a young boy creep up to the bench. He hovered over the sleeping man, carefully removed his glasses, then ran off. I was seized with panic. *When he woke up, how would the man be able to see?* I tried to tell my parents, but the light had changed. We were moving again.

Fifty-plus years later, when I asked my father if he had any memory of this, he said, "Yes, I remember that you were quite excited."

ANYTA

My paternal grandmother was a difficult woman: vain, selfish, opinionated, a spendthrift. At least that's how my mother characterized her; her mother-in-law worked her nerves. Luckily there was some distance between them: We lived in Southern California; my grandparents, in the Bay Area. Certain facts about my grandmother I learned much later, and many years after her death. She was born on the island of Maui in 1906, to Portuguese parents, Francisco and Julia Gonsalves. One of thirteen children, Anna Mary would eventually change her name to Anyta (pronounced "Anita"). Ludvinia, the sister she was closest to, also changed hers, to Lavyne. I like to think they decided to change their names together, after the family had moved stateside, to Oakland, when they were old enough to wear baubles and bob their hair. Where and how she met my grandfather, Rupert Manuel Trinidad, is a mystery. In the sixties, after their three sons were grown, my grandfather's job as an engineer took them to London, where he was involved in the design of the Akosombo Dam in Ghana, and then to Brasília. Though they lived well enough for Anyta to afford a housekeeper, she always wanted more than they had. She liked to entertain, look big. After they returned to the States, they bought a house in a city with a pretty name, Orinda, just east of Berkeley. We visited them there one Christmas. I have a photograph of our family sitting on the mauve silk couch in my grandparents' living room, under a painting of Venice. The couch is long enough to accommodate the six of us: my parents in the middle, flanked on either side by two of their children. My father sports a flattop; my mother, a shocking pink dress. All of us, even my father, are smiling. I was fascinated by the little cloth cocktail napkins my grandmother had brought back from Brazil. Cross-stitched around the edges (with red and green thread), each napkin featured a small embroidered figure: men wearing ponchos and bolero hats, women carrying baskets of fruit over their heads. Stitched underneath each figure, the name of a different South American country: Bolivia, Chile, Paraguay, Brazil. (The napkins are now in my possession: My sisters, who between them had a set of twelve, sent them to me when I said I wanted to write about them.) When I was in high school, we visited my grandparents in Lake Tahoe, where they and Lavyne and her husband owned side-by-side cabins. I remember Anyta sitting at a card table, playing solitaire. Her hair dyed red. On a finger, as she turned over the cards: the big oval amethyst she'd bought in Brazil. Cigarettes and highball (bourbon) nearby. Also: *Look* magazine with Greta Garbo on the cover. *Garbo is 65.* (My age now.) I never heard my grandmother speak Portuguese. The only part of her heritage she shared with us was food: *linguiça* (a spicy sausage) and a braided Christmas bread with bits of colorful dried fruit in it. She outlived my grandfather by sixteen years. When she was dying, at age eighty-six, I went to see her at a nursing home in Hayward, California. "I've had a good life," she said. The nurses didn't like her, my mother told me, because she treated them like the help.

IN THE MIDST OF GRIEF

Barbara Barg died a month or so ago. I was stubbornly unmoved by the news. Why? Residue of disappointment, still, over the time we met, four years ago, for coffee. I ran into her at a Bernadette Mayer reading in Chicago, where we both now lived. I'd known Barbara—not well—in New York in the late eighties, when we were enrolled in the MFA program at Brooklyn College (Barbara in fiction; me, poetry). And now she is dead. Her claim to fame (if you want to call it that): She appeared as a backup singer in Anne Waldman's apocalyptic (and hilariously funny) music video, "Uh-Oh Plutonium!" The best kind of camp: earnestness run amok. Anne desperately wanting to be Patti Smith. Like Ginsberg wanted to be Dylan, with his terrible songs. What I remember most from Allen's Buddhist funeral: that it was uncomfortable sitting on the floor, that Lee Ann Brown was there among the throng. And Anne reading (or ranting) an elegy (written in short order) that ended with "Kind mind don't die, kind mind don't die." I was moved by this, wrote her a note telling her so. In 1983, not long after Ted Berrigan died, Eileen and I visited Alice on St. Mark's Place. An October night. Even the light in that railroad flat seemed to have suffered an enormous loss. Empty spaces on the walls where paintings once hung (sold for needed cash?). Alice complained that *New American Writing* had just accepted her weakest poems. (That's the way with tastemakers: too envious to showcase others at their best.) Anne came up. "The problem with her poems," said Alice, "is that they're too willful." In the midst of grief, time for gossip. But I digress.

Or not. At Bernadette's reading, Barbara and I made a coffee date. Met at Kopi Cafe a few weeks later. Eileen came up. Barbara had heard that I'd read, at my recent Dia reading, a poem about burning Eileen's letters. I explained that I'd burned the letters twenty years earlier, that the poem takes place in the past. On Facebook, Eileen made it sound like I had just burned them. "I'll have to talk to her about that," said Barbara. And then, defensively: "I'm friends with Eileen." I wish I'd said: *I'm not asking you not to be.* She said something about Eileen wanting to control the narrative. I wish I'd said: *Aren't there as many narratives as there are writers?* Her hair was white (in New York it had been black). I never saw her after that. A shame, as we shared an interest in the teachings of Seth. I learned about her death on Facebook.

AUGUST 4, 2018

FIRST DEATH IN SIERRA MADRE

Only I accompanied my mother; I don't know why the rest of the family didn't come. July 1961. I was eight. We attended the viewing, at night, in a small chapel. With my mother's aunts, uncles, and cousins, we sat on the creaky wooden pews and prayed, while Great-grandmother lay in an open casket, brightly lit and immaculately groomed, in a black dress, behind a partition of glass. But where were her spectacles? She who would give me pennies from a little dish on her vanity when we visited her in her house on West Montecito Avenue. I was asked if I wanted to kiss her—that much I remember. If I did, I've blocked it from my mind. The Mass the next morning is also a blank. But I do remember the foliage around Uncle Emile and Aunt Madeline's house: ferns with long thin fronds, leaves with veins like bleeding red ink, heart-shaped elephant ears. The house, half hidden by plants, was white. Terracotta tiles on the roof. Built into the bottom of a wall near the front steps: a tiny grilled door. This is where the milkman would put fresh bottles of milk. There was an identical door on the inside of the house, so the bottles could be removed without having to go out. I thought this magical. In Uncle Emile's den, on a high white shelf: rows of colorfully painted, cast-iron toy soldiers. Is this the origin of my love of miniatures? Skin and hair completely white, Aunt Madeline told me not to touch anything. Her living room full of knickknacks, cut glass, china teacups. And on a table in the center of the room, under a glass dome, a winter scene. More cast-iron figurines: ice skaters on a mirror-pond, horse pulling a sleigh, bobsledders gliding down a hill of glittered cotton. The whole family went out to supper: a long table in a dimly lit restaurant. My mother's cousin Richard (who would come out late in life) ordered me a Shirley Temple: a fizzy pink drink with a maraschino cherry, named after a movie star. That night, on the drive back to Chatsworth, my mother had me lie down in the back seat of our green Ford Falcon, to sleep. But on the freeway she kept calling my name, trying to get me to wake. She was afraid a car was following her, wanted me to sit up. When I did, it immediately veered away.

PALINODE

A POEM IN WHICH THE POET RETRACTS

SOMETHING SAID IN A PREVIOUS POEM

In my book *Answer Song* (1994), I included a prose poem called "Three Deaths," comprised of three paragraph-stanzas. Each recounts a memory of a girl I knew in childhood who died young. The first, Joanne, was a classmate at Superior Street Elementary School in Chatsworth, California, in the 1960s. Thirty years after the fact, I describe her death as I remember it: *She was killed in a traffic accident—along with the driver and a dozen other kids, including the daughter of Roy Rogers and Dale Evans—on the way back from a Christian picnic.* I say that the bus went out of control after hitting a car and ran off a freeway overpass; that I saw, on TV, an image of the crushed, upside-down church bus. I also say that in school Joanne was called a "tomboy" (whereas I was called a "sissy"); that we were in the first grade and sat next to each other; and that the day after her death, someone left flowers, stems wrapped in aluminum foil, on her empty chair.

According to my records, I wrote the poem on January 29, 1992. I was probably still using a typewriter. (The worksheets of the poem are in my papers at the Fales Library in New York, so I can't confirm for sure.) Even if I had a computer by then, I doubt any information about the accident would have been available. The World Wide Web went live six months earlier, on August 6, 1991. Today, twenty-seven years later, Google only brings up a handful of results. Several archived newspaper articles: one from *The New York Times* ("Roy Rogers' Child And 7 Are Killed In Crash of Bus") and one from a Ventura County paper called *The Press-Courier* ("8 die in highway crash; church bus rams 7 cars"). From these articles, I learn the true facts about the accident. It occurred six miles south of San Clemente in Southern California, on August 17, 1964, a Monday, on a stretch of undivided highway dubbed "Slaughter Alley" by locals, for its high number of fatalities. On the bus were sixty-five people, mostly children, members of the Disciples of Christ Chapel of the Canyon Church in Canoga Park. The driver was forty-nine-year-old Rev. Lawrence Elton White. They were returning from a monthly trip to Tijuana, where they had delivered food and clothing to an orphanage. The left front tire blew out, causing the bus to career into oncoming traffic. It struck seven vehicles before coming to rest against a palm tree at the edge of a forty-foot bluff over San Onofre Creek. Highway patrol officer Merrel Kissinger said, "The palm tree may have kept the bus from falling down into the bed. If that had happened, it would have been much worse." Two of the children on the bus were killed: Deborah Lee Rogers (the twelve-year-old adopted Korean daughter of Western film and television stars Roy Rogers and Dale Evans) and her friend, eleven-year-old Joanne Russell, daughter of Mr. and Mrs. Robert Russell of Granada Hills. Debbie and Joanne were standing at the front of the bus, talking with the driver and watching traffic. The other six victims, a family visiting from Albuquerque, New Mexico, were in one station wagon: a twenty-year-old woman, her two infant children, her mother and two sisters. Forty children on the bus were injured; they swarmed out of the rear emergency door screaming and bleeding. All of the seats had come loose in the accident. Children were thrown on the floor, pinned in the wreckage.

On Roy Rogers' Wikipedia page, I read that they lived on a 300-acre ranch near Chatsworth (where we lived), "complete with a hilltop ranch house." After the church bus accident, they moved to Apple Valley, California. I wanted to know more about Joanne's family, the Russells, but couldn't find anything. A subsequent Google search (as I was writing this) uncovered more than I expected. In his 1979 biography of Rogers and Evans, Keith Hunt describes the bus accident in gruesome detail. Debbie was thrown through the windshield and Joanne was jammed beneath the dashboard. Both girls were "terribly mutilated." Dale Evans prolonged telling Roy Rogers the news about their daughter, as he was in the hospital recovering from surgery. Robert Russell drove to San Diego and identified the bodies. Joanne's sister, Kathy, was also on the bus, and severely injured. Right after Joanne's funeral, Robert Russell disappeared. His wife thought he may have driven back East to be with his family. Two weeks later, his car was discovered behind a barn on the Rogers' ranch. He was sitting in it, dead from an overdose of sleeping pills.

In "Three Deaths," I say that the driver and twelve children were killed. Where did that number come from? And why picnic rather than charitable outing? Did someone really put flowers on Joanne's chair? If so, were the stems really wrapped in aluminum foil? Should I trust that exact (and suspiciously poetic) detail when I got some of the most important facts wrong? Hold on: It was summer. School wasn't in session. That's why the children were traveling on a Monday. No one could have left flowers on her chair. "Drawers of memory never full," writes Pierre Reverdy. Like Joanne, I was eleven years old in August 1964. Not in the first grade, but about to start the sixth. This means I would have known Joanne for at least six years. Better than I remember? Roy Rogers was known as "King of the Cowboys." In our family room, I watched repeats of his television show. Did I really see, on the same TV, the crushed church bus? On Find A Grave, I locate Joanne's headstone, which she shares with her father, Robert. (They're buried in Oakwood Memorial Park Cemetery in Chatsworth, less than three miles from where I grew up. Movie stars like Fred Astaire, Gloria Grahame, and Ginger Rogers are also interred there.) "Russell" in all-capital, raised letters across the top. Lit candles on either side, flames casting saintly sunburst rays. Names and dates (written in stone) on facing pages of an open book.

WHY, TODAY, DO I THINK OF MARY,

a girl I barely knew, who, having missed the bus to school, and her parents having already left for work, called a cab company to come fetch her. Nobel Junior High School. Northridge, California. 1966, 67, 68. Mod was all the rage. Mary and the other girls wore white lipstick, Twiggy lashes, blue and green eye shadow. Dresses with puffed sleeves and beribboned lace around the empire waist. Square-toed patent leather shoes with buckles or bows. Textured stockings. And those long, multi-strand plastic necklaces they bought at drug stores and, like flappers, tied into a knot. Nobel had strict dress codes. To prevent girls from wearing minis, they had to kneel on a chair during Homeroom and be measured: Hems weren't allowed to be higher than an inch above the knee. How many risked punishment in order to be hip? Why, today, do I think of this? I, who was forced to take Woodshop and Drafting when I would much rather have learned to cook and sew in Home Ec. I might have become a chef, a costume designer for the movies. Aren't I happy with who I am? Poet. Professor. Connoisseur of lost worlds. I thought Mary's action showed great ingenuity. But when a teacher saw her get out of a taxi in front of school, she was carted off to the principal's office.

RAY DONOVAN

On a frigid night in late November 2018, my coach house in Chicago surrounded by icy snow, I watch the first episode of *Ray Donovan* and am delighted to see, during the credits, that the series was created by Ann Biderman. Her name a Proustian madeleine: Thirty years evaporate like so much wintry mist. In 1988, on the verge of moving from Los Angeles to New York, I dog-sat for her in the house she shared with her partner, director Roger Vadim, in Santa Monica. We'd met through Raymond Foye, who published me in his Hanuman series: colorful, pocket-sized books, inspired by Indian prayer books, that were printed in Madras. An aspiring screenwriter, Ann was petite and pretty, with long black hair and an air of authority that comes, I imagined, from hobnobbing with celebrities. She gave me a recipe that Jane Fonda had given her: a blended drink made from boiled greens that she subsisted on while filming movies, to keep her weight down. Ann's dog was named Genius, a sweet, long-legged mutt with grayish fur and a goofy face. At night when I got into bed, Genius would set his head on the edge of the mattress and stare at me with soulful eyes. I wrote a little poem about him that said just that. Stacks of books everywhere; it felt like I was being embraced by my future life. I sat at the dining table and typed letters to the poets I would hang out with in New York: Tim, Jimmy, Joe, Elaine, Eileen. The cottage-like house was nestled in the hills overlooking the Pacific. Steep concrete steps led up to it from the street. Small yard. Low chain-link fence. I was instructed to keep the gate closed at all times, so Genius wouldn't get out. Donald Britton visited me while I was staying there. I served him tea and cookies. He had just moved from New York to Los Angeles. We joked that we were poets passing in the night, so to speak; trading places; that by each of us moving across the country at the same time, in opposite directions, we were keeping the scales balanced. But only for a moment. Donald died of AIDS before finishing a second book. While I've had time to write many. I hadn't been in New York long when Raymond told me that a subsequent dog-sitter left the gate open: Genius had made his way down to the street and was killed by a car.

After the reverie wears off, I send Ann a friend request on Facebook. And learn, on Wikipedia, that the pages of Raymond's Hanuman books were stitched by local fishermen in Madras.

NOT JUST IN MEMORY

Awake from a nap, I notice, in the bookcase beside my bed, the orangish-brown spine of a book I've owned for more than forty years. By Anna Seldis. In the fall of 1972, a shy, nineteen-year-old student at Cal State Northridge, I took a Modern Italian Literature course with her. Only a few of us enrolled, so we met each week in her small office in Sierra Tower. We read *The Conformist, The Garden of the Finzi-Continis,* Italo Calvino's *Cosmicomics,* poems by Eugenio Montale. The intimacy of the setting, and the trust Anna engendered, enabled me to come out of myself, express my opinions. She gave me an A (my only other that semester was in Folk Dance). I kept in touch the next couple of years, showed her my first poems. She was encouraging, though they must have been awful. (Later I'd burn those early efforts in my parents' fireplace.) I bought her book, *I cieli per noi sono tetto (The Skies Are Our Roof)*—a bilingual edition, printed in Italy, with plain orangish-brown cover—which she inscribed, on May 15, 1975, "To David, one of my very special students"—the reason I've kept it all these years. The poem I liked best was "A Nightmare at the College" because I could tell she was writing about the eight-story tower where we had met for class: "the elevator crashes / down to the ground." Is she still alive? I don't want to look her up on the Internet. Want her to live only in what I remember. She was married to the art critic for the *Los Angeles Times.* What else? Oh yes, she had a captivating accent.

I couldn't help myself: I looked her up. *Non solo nella memoria.* She'd also written a cookbook of Italian desserts—I'd forgotten that. *La Dulce Cucina (The Sweet Kitchen).* It turns out her husband, Henry Seldis, who'd fled Nazi Germany as a teenager (his Jewish father owned one of the biggest umbrella factories in Berlin before the war); studied journalism at Columbia; and become a critic, lecturer, and author (*Henry Moore in America*), committed suicide in 1978. On the eve of his fifty-third birthday. He'd been depressed since Anna started divorce proceedings, had previously attempted an overdose. They had a son named Mark (who would go on to be an associate producer of the movie *Dead Man Walking*). Anna then married Sidney W. Benson, a chemist and professor at USC. They remained together for twenty-six years, until his death at ninety-three. Anna published two more cookbooks and, in 2011, a novel, *The Lion and the Swastika*, based on her own experience: *A young girl faces the cruelty of war in Nazi-occupied Venice.* I couldn't find any contact information for her online, but it looks like Anna is still alive.

OPAL

The family stories are mixed in with my own dim memories. My parents knew Opal, my godmother, from Albuquerque in the early 1950s. Opal had designs on Larry, my mother's stepfather, who owned the paint store where my parents first met. I have a scratched black-and-white snapshot of my mother standing in front of the store, wearing a dark skirt and white sweater, and lipstick (undoubtedly red), her posture and smile constrained. Even young, my mother looked mature. In the window are some unfinished figurines (rooster, ruffled calypso dancer) and cans of Olympic paint. My parents were both students at UNM. Larry chose Ann, who loved dogs (boxers). They had one son, Neil, who would drink himself to death as an adult. Opal married Joe, a plumbing contractor whose first wife had died. After my father graduated, my parents relocated to Southern California, as did a number of their friends, including Opal and Joe. According to my father, Opal was bossy, ran everything behind the scenes. Joe was large, a rough, big-handed guy. My father liked him. Joe would kid with people. If he patted you on the back, he'd almost knock you over. This must be why I, as a child, felt terrorized by my godfather; my only memory of him is his crushing handshake. Joe's death, as reported by my mother: He got up in the middle of the night to go to the bathroom and dropped dead of a heart attack. Opal was never the same. Became overly religious. She was the source of an early spiritual crisis. My beloved pet guinea pig, Checkers, had died. At a Christmas gathering, I sat next to "Aunt" Opal on the couch in our living room, told her that I said prayers for Checkers every night, imagined him up in Heaven with God. She instructed me that animals do not go to Heaven, as they do not have souls. Only humans have souls. Animals just go into the dirt. This threw me into confusion. Thereafter I never fully believed in the Catholic God. When I was a teenager, I chose, at my mother's suggestion, Joseph as my confirmation name. To please Opal. She gave me a ceramic statue of St. Joseph—cumbersome (about a foot high); his draped robe was brown. My mother would have a falling-out with Opal. About politics. Opal no longer came to our holiday dinners.

Years later, when my parents moved from the Valley, they wanted to get rid of the bedroom set Opal had loaned them after Joe died. My mother contacted Opal, who'd been diagnosed with cancer. Did she want the set back or did she want them to sell it and send her the money? Opal chose the latter. They sold it for $250.00. (There's more to say about this bed set. I was raped on it when I was eighteen. I've never told the story in its entirety. A story that ties into, it occurs to me now, several family secrets. How my mother intimated she'd been molested by her cousin George, who was killed in World War II. How Larry had apparently touched her inappropriately after her mother died. *You're as pretty as Marguerite.* How Neil and I played around when we visited Larry and

Ann in Miami when I was twelve. To be explored, possibly, in another poem.) My father remembers the bed set as "reddish wood, dark, depressing." I remember it as baroque.

Opal chain-smoked. Wore glasses. Was plain. Something odd about her nostrils—pronounced, inflamed. Cigarette smoke streamed from them. After my mother sent Opal the check for the bed set, my sister Jenny and I met with her, at a Bob's Big Boy or a chain pie restaurant—neither of us can remember which. We hadn't seen her in at least fifteen years; by then I was in my early thirties. She said: "Don't smoke."

In Miami, Larry was a bookkeeper for a "wheeler-dealer" (my father can't recall his name) who bought and sold stocks and companies. Larry had a laundromat on the side that Ann basically ran. Jenny remembers Ann as unattractive. Into crafts: made quilts, restrung old beads into necklaces. Her marriage to Larry haunted by the memory of his dead first wife, my mother's pretty mother. Ann couldn't compete with the mystique of Marguerite.

WINONA RYDER

I never understood everyone's indignation when she was arrested for shoplifting. The poor woman was obviously in crisis. And besides, she's a movie star, why shouldn't she be allowed to shoplift? She'd already given her soul to celluloid, so to speak. The satisfaction of seeing a mighty one fall, I guess. I've always thought her 480 hours of community service would have made a great reality TV show. What a missed opportunity. Winona helping blind children, caring for babies with AIDS. Oscar worthy! Or at least Emmy. She was ordered to complete her hours of service at the City of Hope medical center. City of Hope!

FREEWRITE AFTER BREATHING, LAST CLASS, 12/11/18

Breathe in the smell of cookies. (I got my pink star.) Breathe through the two women talking in the hall. I heard one say "suffered a lot" and later "stay home with the dog." I wonder what's going to happen on *Ray Donovan* tonight. Last night, right before going to bed, he shot a Russian in the head. What an image to fall asleep to. Dreamt Ted Hughes told me that my writing about Plath was "sensitive and engaging." "Yours, too," I said. We were in a talk show-like setting. Someone just coughed. I've taken a few bites of the pink star. It's now half a star. Now it's a fourth. It has peppermint sprinkles on it.

"THE HAPPIEST PLACE ON EARTH"

Leaving the park, I would buy rock candy at the Candy Palace on Main Street. Last stop at the end of a long and exhausting (albeit magical) day. It came in a clear plastic box with a hinged lid and gold lettering. A little box of sweet white crystals that I could suck on the silent drive home. Over the years, I've collected bits of memorabilia: a map of Tom Sawyer's Island, a wooden nickel from Frontierland, a silver Tinker Bell charm. A dozen Disneykins—I had them as a child—tiny, colorful, hand-painted figures. My favorite was Alice, in her blue dress and white pinafore. Several oversized maps of the entire park, one of which, framed, hangs in the stairway of my coach house. I pass it numerous times every day. Fantasyland was where I most wanted to be—"the happiest land of all." I loved the Alice in Wonderland ride, though the fall down the rabbit hole wasn't as dramatic as I would have liked. Peter Pan's flight over London at night was always enchanting. And the part in Mr. Toad's Wild Ride where you enter a dark tunnel and a train comes speeding toward you, always scary. Did I scream like the other children? My friend Jeffery recently told me that the Mr. Toad attraction no longer exists at the Magic Kingdom. All things must vanish, but not Mr. Toad! The merry-go-round and flying elephants were for kids. The spinning teacups could make you sick, especially if you'd eaten a tuna fish sandwich at the restaurant on Captain Hook's ship (sponsored by Chicken of the Sea, the brand with a mermaid on the can). You could get your name stitched on a felt hat, though I never did. I envied the languid plumes that adorned them. As a child, Jeffery was terrified of going through the whale's mouth, the portal to Storybook Land—all those miniature imaginary dwellings along a canal. "To your right are the houses of the three little pigs," the guide "steering" the boat would announce. There was Gepetto's workshop. And there, at the top of a hill, Cinderella's pink castle.

I still have the little glass slipper I bought the last time I was there. Keep it in a small blue Tiffany's box, like a piece of valuable jewelry. I regret that I gave away, in the eighties, a souvenir my brother got in Adventureland when we were young: a black plastic tiki god pendant, with two red rhinestones for eyes.

LAST POEM

FOR MICHAEL ROBINS

It's Sylvia Plath's death day and I'm writing this on her "little glasstopped table," a table that was actually in her apartment when she died. (I won it in a Bonhams auction last spring.) She describes it in one of her late letters: "straw & black iron, in which I can put flowerpots & currently have a lilac hyacinth." I just reread "Edge," possibly her last poem. (She wrote another, "Balloons," on the same day.) Is it her death poem? Sounds like it: "The woman is perfected." And that "smile of accomplishment" I suddenly find haunting. *All - is the price of All -*. I wonder if I will die with a sense of satisfaction. I've been told, by a psychic, that I will. But will I have time to write my death poem? Tim Dlugos did ("D.O.A."): "Not so bad / for the dead." Raymond Carver has "Late Fragment." Ted Berrigan has "Last Poem," but I don't think it really was his last. In fact, I know it wasn't. "Let none regret my end who called me friend." H.D. wrote her own "Epitaph" before she left. And Allen, "Death & Fame." Just had to have the final word, didn't he. In his death poem, Bashō dreamt of withered fields. Issa kept his wit till the last: "A bath when you're born, / a bath when you die, / how stupid." It's frigid in Chicago. There's snow on the ground like there was in London in February 1963. Of course Sylvia has an answer to that: "The snow has no voice." William Carlos Williams' collected ends with what seems like a death poem: "Sooner or later / we must come to the end / of striving." I wonder what poem will end mine. I just reread "Balloons." Strange to think of the table in my living room as "dead furniture." Yet Sylvia put live flowers in it! Last week I asked my accountant if the table, or any part of it (shipping was a third of the total cost), was deductible. His response: "Well, I suppose you could say that it inspires you. But no."

FEBRUARY 11, 2019

DAVID TRINIDADS

Before the Internet, there was only one David Trinidad. Me. Now there are seemingly thousands. Google brings up any number of them. One David Trinidad is a nurse practitioner in Richland, Washington. Another David Trinidad plays varsity soccer at Cherokee High School in Canton, Georgia. He is 5´8″ and weighs 165 lbs.; his jersey number is 1. He will graduate in 2019. In April 2006, David Trinidad, age eighteen, was convicted of "aggravated battery causing great bodily harm with hate crime enhancements" in Santa Fe, New Mexico. In February of the previous year, he and five others beat a young gay man into a coma outside La Quinta Inn "because of his sexuality." Ironic, to say the least, given I am an openly gay poet. Who is this doppelgänger, this David Trinidad from the dark side? The attackers met up outside the Denny's where Trinidad worked as a waiter. Ninety-year-old David Trinidad, who after serving in the army during World War II pursued a career as a mason, "went to be with the Lord" on March 13, 2018. In Milpitas, California, David Trinidad is a salesperson at Ashley Homestore. Says one customer review: "We purchased mattress and a sofa lounge here at Ashley with the great assistance and help from David Trinidad." In the Dominican Republic, David Trinidad is a producer and DJ who has released several albums on his own label, OMG Music. I just listened to his "I Need You! (Original Mix)" on YouTube. At first I liked it, but then it started to give me a headache (relentless beat).

On Facebook, there is an endless scroll of David Trinidads. One is a fire-fighter who studied at Malcolm X College. One is a maintenance technician at Boulevard Brewing Company in Kansas City, Missouri. One lives in Chicago (as I do) and is a Cubs fan (which I am not). One is obese (his profile picture is a selfie). One (cowboy hat, mustache) sits astride a white horse. One likes fishing; another, basketball. There are several David Trinidads in the Naked City (New York), where I used to live. (I knew I wouldn't be missed. But so copiously replaced?) There's one in Jacksonville, Florida. One in Racine, Wisconsin. One in South Australia. Texas. Mexico City. El Salvador. Peru. Uruguay. Argentina. Pennsylvania. New Jersey. Ohio. South Bend, Indiana. And on and on.

A David Trinidad once sent me an email that said, "I see you're famous. I'm going to be famous too." I believe he was a photographer. I'm the only poet named David Trinidad that I know of, though there may be others out there, lurkers hungry for recognition. As of this date (March 12, 2019), I am the only David Trinidad with a Wikipedia page.

MEMOIR

Another Friday night at Beyond Baroque, circa 1982. Anne Waldman is at the worn black podium, reciting a poem. Her reading style is incantatory, but forced. An unseen heckler begins to goad her, from the back of the room. Lewis MacAdams jumps to Anne's defense, threatening violence. An intense moment, then the poem continues. Afterward there's a party, as there usually is, at Sheree's house on Thurston Avenue in Brentwood—hers after her divorce—where she lives with her two teenaged children and her poet-performer boyfriend, Bob Flanagan. Bob has drawn Sheree into the world of S&M. From well-to-do Jewish housewife to dominatrix. From cystic fibrosis to supermasochist. That story. I smoke in the yellow kitchen, wait for provisions (beer and potato chips) to arrive. Bob puts Wall of Voodoo on the stereo in the living room: "I fell into a burning ring of fire." Kate Braverman (all in black) makes a rare appearance, to chat up Anne Waldman, and is flabbergasted that Waldman has never heard of her. "Why, I'm the grande dame of the Los Angeles poetry scene!" The best kind of fodder for the gossip mill: poets blind to the size of their own ego. Because we often run out of alcohol by the time the liquor stores are closed (2:00 a.m.), I hide, while there's still plenty, a six-pack under the sink in the back bathroom; that way I always have a beer in hand, which I pretend to nurse, lest someone become suspicious of my stash. (Years later I'll learn that Ed Smith had his own hiding place for same.) Those parties sometimes lasted all weekend. I'd stay on, till Saturday, till Sunday afternoon, afraid to drive drunk (post-accident). Afraid of sitting alone in my Hollywood hovel, too depressed to write the new poems I desperately wanted to write. Distressed about returning, Monday morning, to the Housing Authority, a job I was ill-suited for. It felt safe at Sheree's. Bob would walk around naked, on acid, weights hanging from his balls. Sheree would brag about the size of her son's cock. I'd lay in their bed, head aching, watching the colorized version of *It's a Wonderful Life* on TV. Wondering if the world would be any different without me.

One Sunday morning (January 16, 1983, to be exact), I sat with Celia Pearce in the breakfast nook and typed the collaboration we'd just written, "Ed Smith Slept Here." Which we dedicated to our host; Sheree was a den mother of sorts. Then Celia and I read it out loud, alternating lines: "How can we even think of breakfast / When we haven't even begun to live." If Gail Kaszynski hadn't filmed us reading and talking (and uploaded it, thirty-three years later, on YouTube), I'd never have remembered that when I visited Alice Notley on St. Mark's Place the previous October (my first trip to New York), I brought her a bouquet of pink and white carnations. And a six-pack. One sunny, hungover morning, I sat on Sheree's front lawn and talked with Lynne Tillman (the reader at Beyond Baroque that week; I loved her short story about Marilyn Monroe). We both wore sunglasses. I asked her about New York—where I desperately wanted to live, to live the writer's life. (I would one day, but not until after

I got sober. Lynne would be a friend in the years I lived there.) Another morning, I sat on the lawn with Jane DeLynn. Her cutting wit intimidated me. But Tim Dlugos (whom I adored) adored her. And we had the same sign (Cancer). When I asked her to inscribe *In Thrall*, her second novel, she wrote, "To David and his beautiful hair."

JOANNE KYGER

The straight white bangs were a sign that a little girl lurked inside of the mature woman. A mischievous, or better, bratty, little girl. *In a supermarket: mother with out-of-control child. Child kicks Joanne. Joanne kicks child back. Mother not very happy about that.* Her inner girl liked to have a good time. In 2010, at an impromptu party in her motel room after a poetry reading at Naropa, she insisted that we all sing. "What's your favorite song?" she kept prodding us. When several people finally started singing "Don't Explain," she tried, like an eager little girl, to follow along. But was too looped to keep up with the lyrics. In poems, she was committed to accurately notating the mind at play in the present moment. The particular always gave way to something larger. At the podium she had a regal presence. Delivered her words emphatically, like a fervid minister. She even looked the part. Long gold scarf draped over loose black clothing. Gold chains. Hoop earrings. She wore her sunglasses when she read. (You could only see into her through the poems.) I admired her greatly. A line from *The Wonderful Focus of You* actually changed the way I look at life: "Time is a nice thing to go through." I sent her my books over the years, and each time she responded with a gracious note. "So wonderful ... and what a breeze to read." "I love your new book." She read one by flashlight when electricity was out in Bolinas for a week, and found it "delightful company." In 2007, when *The Late Show* came out, we read together at Moe's Books in Berkeley. November 6, a Tuesday. D.A. Powell accompanied me from San Francisco. We had dinner with Joanne and her partner Donald at a macrobiotic Thai restaurant on Telegraph Avenue (Joanne's choice; she was strict about her diet), then walked down the street to the bookstore. Her friend Cedar Sigo was there. I tried to strike up a conversation, but he seemed jittery, repeatedly mentioned his boyfriend. *My boyfriend, my boyfriend, my boyfriend.* Did he think I was coming on to him? I was just being friendly because I'd read and liked some of his poems. The reading was downstairs. An aunt and cousin, who lived in San Rafael, unexpectedly showed up. I felt especially vulnerable with relatives in the front row. I went first, and made a point of saying what an honor it was to read with Joanne. The next day, a gracious email: "Such a pleasure to read with you last night and have a chance to chat a bit with you and Doug before the reading." When Tony Trigilio brought her to Chicago to read in a Beat festival at Columbia College, I saw another side of Joanne. Before the reading, she was obsessed with the lighting, kept directing the tech assistant to readjust it. She didn't want the sign language interpreter to stand too close to the podium. Didn't want the flowers too close, either. Did she fear they'd upstage her? I sat next to her in the audience. Still perturbed about the lighting, she talked right through Tony's introduction. Smart and admiring, he'd labored over it. But Joanne didn't hear a word. She did, to her credit, email him later and apologize, ask to see a copy of it. Tony referred to her as "the angry

Buddhist." (All Buddhists have a problem with anger, my ex-partner used to say.) As affable as she was, I was aware, the few times I was with her, of an undercurrent of disquiet.

In Joanne's *Collected Poems*, which I had her sign at the Thai restaurant in Berkeley, I inserted the BART receipt from Doug's and my trek from San Francisco. Van, who I knew from AA in Chicago, had come to the reading. He gave us a ride back to the city. Van who was sexually abused by his older sister throughout his adolescence. Who would relapse shortly after I saw him on that trip. I haven't heard from him since.

"ORDINARY TIME"

My first two weeks in New York (August 1988), Raymond Foye let me stay at his apartment on Ninth Street (near Sixth Avenue) until my sublet in Brooklyn was ready. The apartment actually belonged to art figure Henry Geldzahler (whom I'd met earlier that year with Raymond when they showed me the pool David Hockney had painted at the Hollywood Roosevelt Hotel). Raymond's bedroom was on the basement level, along with the laundry room, kitchen, dining area, and living room, which opened on a dark, walled-in garden. Art covered all of the walls. In Raymond's room there was a small Warhol—one of his flower paintings; I felt privileged to sleep in the same room with it. In the living room, the TV sat on a Brillo Box. Raymond was with Henry on Long Island, so I had the place to myself. Eileen visited me there. She showed me her poem "Hot Night" and the little essay she'd written about it. I was entranced (being brand new in New York) by the idea of stepping out into the night, into the city, "of going out to get a poem, like hunting." Tim Dlugos also visited me there. After admiring the art, he drove me (in his mother's car; she'd died of leukemia the previous year) to New Haven, where he had just moved to attend Yale Divinity School. He wanted me to see his new living quarters (the bottom floor of a house on Rowe Street). We ate lunch in town. I bought a gray T-shirt with "Yale" on it.

I'd grown my hair long and, in my left ear, sported a gold stud. (Before I left L.A., Bob Flanagan pierced it for me. I recently learned that there are photographs of the piercing in Sheree Rose's archive at USC; I'd forgotten she documented it.) The following spring, Tim would commemorate my Yale T-shirt and long hair in "Ordinary Time," a poem about going out to eat after an AA meeting in Manhattan; both Eileen and I appear in it. More importantly, though, it's about the intensity (and clarity) of the "eternal present"—the spiritual awareness that frees him from the confines of ordinary time. Tim captures, in words, the magic ("something / that shines through the things / I make and do and say"), and the momentary communion among friends. All well and good for him. But not enough light for me to see the dark road ahead. My enmity with Eileen. (When I sought Tim's counsel, he was in the AIDS ward at Roosevelt Hospital. "Well," he said, "Eileen can be prickly.") Then the finality of Tim's death.

Back at Raymond's, I wrote my first poem as a resident of New York, "Driving Back from New Haven," about a moment on the Merritt Parkway when, after taking an AZT pill ("'Poison,' he mutters under his breath"), Tim and I discuss his health. I wrote it because Michael Klein asked me for work for an AIDS anthology. I sent it to Tim first, with a note: "Please like this." "Was I really that angry?" he asked. But gave his blessing. One morning, I made a cup of tea and set it on Geldzahler's mid-century modern dining table. Blond wood. It left a circle—a permanent stain—which I obsessed about. Ultimately I didn't say anything, moved to Brooklyn hoping they wouldn't notice, or not know that I was the careless houseguest who had left the mark.

Last month, thirty years after Tim wrote "Ordinary Time," I received a postcard from Walter Holland: "Happy 50th Pride! Went to hear Stonewall Legacy Reading of Poetry last night in Bryant Park. Don Yorty read Tim Dlugos' 'Ordinary Time' & I thought of you & Eileen Myles & East Village days."

1968

The porchlight will be on, waiting for me, when I come home from babysitting. Almost every Saturday night I sit for a couple who live one street over from us, at the end of a cul-de-sac. The wife teaches ballet. The husband is handsome. They have two young girls. I am fifteen years old. I earn money babysitting (and also mow lawns) so I can buy books about the movies. *The Films of Greta Garbo*. *The Films of Marilyn Monroe*. *Judy: The Films and Career of Judy Garland*. *The Academy Awards: A Pictorial History*. The girls have Barbie dolls. I watch them play. Even pick up a doll and slip her into a dress; it's safe, in this context. After they go to sleep, I sit in an armchair in the family room and watch *Mannix* on their TV. Mike Connors has dark hair and is handsome, like the husband. Then I watch Cinema 13 (on channel 13), the only place you can see adult-themed movies (albeit edited): *The Pawnbroker* (about a concentration camp survivor), *Mondo Cane* (shocking), *90° in the Shade* (steamy), *A Taste of Honey* (about a pregnant teenager), *One Potato, Two Potato* (about an interracial relationship). When the couple comes home, the husband always drives me to my house. Why? It's only a block and a half away. The world is a dangerous place, but surely our suburb is still safe. Does his wife insist? What do we talk about, if anything, on that short drive. I can smell cigarettes, alcohol on his breath—they've been to a party. I look over at his profile, lit by the dashboard, framed in the window like a leading man. Houses glide past, in darkness, behind him.

Our house is yellow. The porchlight glows. The handsome husband waits for me to turn the key and go inside, before he drives off.

DIGGING TO WONDERLAND

Nancy knocks on our front door, tears streaming down her face. "Char-
lotte is dead!" She's just finished reading *Charlotte's Web* and is devas-
tated that Wilbur has lost his best friend. The DeMarios live five doors
down from us on Comanche Avenue. Their house is pale blue. I knock
on Nancy's bedroom window and she pops up, face streaked with tears.
She's listening to her *Meet the Beatles!* album. The British Invasion has
reached California; it's 1964. Soon Nancy will move from Chatsworth to
Thousand Oaks, and I will be devastated. For seven years (age five to
twelve) she was my best friend. (We're still, miraculously, in our mid-
sixties, in touch with each other.) Six months older than me, taller, unruly
black hair, in her striped sunsuit and flip-flops, protective like a big sister,
the leader in all things. We played school (alternating being the teacher),
wrote and put on plays in her backyard (hung beach towels on a clothes-
line for curtains). Gave funerals for insects and birds, placed their match-
box or shoebox coffins in a red wagon (with snapdragons from my
mother's flowerbed) and led a solemn procession down the sidewalk, bu-
ried them (reciting prayers) in one or the other's yard. After seeing the
Rose Parade on TV, we longed for a float. Her father (an engineer like
mine) let us decorate his car with pink toilet paper flowers, and drove us
around the neighborhood. Nancy, wearing a black slip (her gown) and
red lipstick, leaned out the window and waved at the other children. (I
sat back, too shy.) Our greatest adventure was when we tried to dig a hole

to Wonderland. We'd both, of course, read *Alice in Wonderland* (and seen the Disney movie) several times. A friend of our family, Seyvella (married to Nobert, also an engineer), who worked at the Disney Studios in Burbank, gave us some stills from the movie. One, a map of Wonderland, mesmerized me. It showed the path that Alice took after she fell down the rabbit hole, pictured all the goofy characters she met along the way: Tweedledum and Tweedledee, the talking flowers, the smoke-blowing Caterpillar, the Mad Hatter, Cheshire Cat, and, at the end of a maze of hedges, the bellowing Queen of Hearts. Nancy and I would create a Wonderland of our own, underneath her backyard. We'd dug a fairly deep hole, and were about to start shoveling sideways, when Nancy's mother realized what we were up to. Mary, a bohemian stuck in suburbia, wore sleeveless blouses and pedal pushers, smoked cigarettes continually, read countless books. She became agitated at the thought that our tunnel might cave in and suffocate us, and made us fill it in.

Nancy remembers that there was something about the way we played, our uninhibited creativity and ability to immerse ourselves in make-believe, that scared others and that they wanted us to suppress. She says that in elementary school, I was miserable when I was removed from class once a week to see the school psychologist. Because it drew attention to me. (I was already in speech class—to correct a lisp.) They had me see the psychologist because I was interested in softer things, feminine things, playing with girls, fantasy and fairy tales. Initially I was ambidextrous, but they trained me to use only my right hand.

THAT WAS ALLEN

IN RESPONSE TO A QUESTIONNAIRE
ABOUT ALLEN GINSBERG'S TEACHING
METHODS AND THEIR EFFECTIVENESS

I studied with Allen my first year in the MFA program at Brooklyn College (1988–89). A workshop in the fall and spring, and weekly tutorials in his office at school. I actually applied to Brooklyn because the poet Joan Larkin was there. She'd written a book of poems about sobriety and I very much wanted to study with a sober poet. (I'd gotten sober five years earlier.) Everyone assumed I came to study with Allen (who was still, I believe, filling in for John Ashbery, who never returned), but that was not the case. I always entertained some ambivalence about Allen, more so as a person/figure than as a poet. I'd read him as an undergraduate and admired his work, though I wouldn't count him as a key influence. I was much more interested in the Confessional poets (Sexton and Plath), and by the time I studied with Allen, the New York School poets (Schuyler, Brainard, Notley, and Berrigan). He once passed out a list of recommended poets/books—a single page crowded with typed and handwritten suggestions—which I wish I'd saved. Blake and Whitman were on it. And Kerouac and Corso, of course, the usual suspects. He pushed John Wieners, in particular, felt that he should be better known than he was. The only women on the list were Sappho and Anne Waldman. That didn't sit well with me, as I admired many female poets. I wish I'd been more open to reading the poets on Allen's list. But I was pretty dug in, aesthetically, in that phase of my life. And Allen was pretty set in his ways, too; it made me resist his tastes, rather than embrace them. I've said this before (but that won't keep me from saying it again): He was not at all sympathetic to what I was trying to do. If you mimicked his style, he praised you. I suppose he taught me that I didn't want the kind of fame he espoused. I didn't want to be a victim of, or addicted to, fame. He wore his faults on his sleeve—there for all to see. So there was this nakedness about him, perhaps even vulnerability, despite his fame-mind. He was always dogmatic about poetics, though.

I seem to remember him being a little impatient and/or bored, in general. Outside of class he was warmer, more relaxed. He held several classes at his apartment on the Lower East Side, or maybe they were end-of-semester parties. At one of these, he pulled from his bookshelf my second book of poems, which I'd sent him from Los Angeles several years earlier. He removed my note from it, and pointed out that I'd not dated it. "Always date everything," he advised. I have ever since. He also made a big deal about writing with a good pen (fountain) on good paper. I think he said he got this notion from Rimbaud—the poet's holy paraphernalia. He often repeated "first thought, best thought," emphasized looseness, keeping the words flowing. He once said, "Every line should have a shimmer." I've never forgotten that. I remember how much I liked "May

Days 1988" when it was first published. Allen's honesty about aging. I'm sure I told him so. He signed books for me, such generous inscriptions. I have a photograph of some of us at one of the gatherings at his apartment: Paul Beatty, Pamela Hughes, Karen Kelley (and child), and me, wearing my orange Brooklyn College T-shirt. And one of me and Allen at St. Mark's Church the night of the big Hanuman Books reading in 1989. He is striking his stoic pose. I'm almost smiling.

It was either naive or brazen of me, but I asked Allen if he would be a recommender for a Guggenheim application. This was over the phone. He bluntly said, "I really don't get [he might have said 'like'] what you're doing, Trinidad. I'd much rather support someone like Antler. But go ahead, put me down." I didn't, out of pride. Antler visited one of our workshops. I liked some of his poems, but overall felt he was too derivative of Allen, and too excessive. I suppose, on some level, I wanted Allen's praise, but wouldn't have been able to admit or acknowledge that to myself. I was meeting with James Schuyler once a week at the Chelsea Hotel; he was much more of a mentor.

My second year of grad school, I was slotted to study with Susan Fromberg Schaeffer, a writer that I did not admire in the least. I believe she started the MFA program at Brooklyn with Ashbery. She was a bad poet who gave up poetry to write bad novels. I tried to get out of working with her, tried to stay in Allen's workshop. He wouldn't allow it, said he'd taught me everything he had to teach me. So I was stuck with Susan. She presided over the workshop like a member of the Addams Family: dyed black hair, black robe-like getups, glasses thick as Mason jars. She relied on me to start a good many of the class discussions (critiques of my peers' poems). Then gave me—slap in the face—a B in the course. It turns out she'd given B's to *all* of the gay and lesbian students in the class. (She'd once lamented, "Confessionalism is running rampant on this campus!" I suspected this was a veiled reference to a poem I'd written for Allen's class, a litany of past lovers, that had caused a bit of controversy—it was explicit.) Because of this, and because I'd essentially co-taught the workshop, I filed a grievance about the grade, citing homophobia. One day I ran into Allen in the hall and he said, rather aggressively, "Why are you doing this? Don't you know it's bad karma!" Maybe he'd been asked to weigh in on the matter, and felt put on the spot. I probably clammed up. Though I'm sure I didn't see what could be bad, karmically, about standing up for oneself. The grade wasn't changed, ultimately, but a few years later the director of the program told Joan Larkin that he thought it had been homophobia on Susan's part. That was vindication, of sorts.

AUGUST 13, 2019

MYSTERY HOUSE MAGNET

Three days after an event for our dead friend Ed Smith, celebrating a collection of his poems and notebooks, which I edited, Amy and I drive from Los Angeles to San Francisco. June 2019. If he hadn't committed suicide in 2005, Ed would be sixty-two. Amy and I have been friends for almost forty years. I'd planned to keep a travel diary of our trip, but the last few days have been jam-packed: the Ed event at Beyond Baroque (followed by dinner with Jimm and Celeste), a day in the Valley with my old friend David (which included a pilgrimage to my childhood home), two interviews (one about my poems, one about Ed's) for Michael Silverblatt's Bookworm, "the country's premier literary talk-show." My head is spinning, a bit, from this "rock star" pace. It was old home week at Beyond Baroque. Friends I hadn't seen in decades read Ed's work: James Krusoe, Bill Mohr, Jack Skelley. Just hours before the reading, we learned that another Los Angeles poet from the past, Holly Prado, had died at the age of eighty-one. In tribute, I read one of her poems (which I found on the Internet) at the start of the event: "Paper," an elegy for yet another poet from the old days, Wanda Coleman: "Another poet died / last week, a presence I have counted on for forty years . . . I can't do anything for death." At dinner afterward, as Jimm and Celeste and I sat on the patio of a cafe off Venice Boulevard, we witnessed a car crash. My cell phone rang as the ambulance arrived: Michael Silverblatt, to tell me he'd heard that Kevin Killian had died. Kevin who was scheduled to read at another event for Ed (the purpose of Amy's and my trip north) at City Lights Books in a couple of days. Amy and I stop for an hour at my father's house in the Central Coast—just long enough for her to meet him and my sister Jennifer (and the two dogs: Biscuit and Wally), for us to use the bathroom, and for me to make a peanut butter sandwich for the road. As we proceed up the coast, I remember (out loud) the many times I drove from L.A. to San Francisco in the eighties: to read for Kevin when he ran the series at Small Press Traffic (I was supposed to read with Sam D'Allesandro, but he was too ill—dying of AIDS—so Robert Glück took his place), to be the guest of honor at a party Kevin threw (at which no one, except Harold Norse, spoke to me), to attend Kevin and Dodie's wedding. I remember during one visit going to see *Aliens* with Kevin and Steve Abbott, and how scary the movie was. I remember that Kevin smoked Parliaments, that he always drank Tab. I remember Kevin and Dodie's Victorian wedding cake: white, three-tiered, with lavender flowers (and not as sweet, I thought, as it looked). I remember the last time I spent time with Kevin—at a writers conference in Maine in June 2017. After he read, I told him his poems were "fucking brilliant." I'm glad that that was our last in-person interaction, and that he'd recently written, via email, a nice blurb for Ed's book. We pass San Juan Bautista, where scenes from Alfred Hitchcock's *Vertigo* were shot, and I remember that Amy and I went to see it when it was rereleased in the eighties (it hadn't been available for many years; I had vivid memories of watching it on the late show in my teens and being traumatized when Kim Novak falls to her death at the end). As we approach San Jose, I notice a sign for the Winchester Mystery House. Another memory: stopping there, in the early nineties, when Ira and Bob and Sheree and I made this drive (Bob and I were to read, along with Dorothy Allison and Wanda Coleman, for Ira's *High Risk* anthology at a gallery in San Francisco). The haunted house a perfect metaphor for my friendship with Sheree and Bob: a stairway that leads nowhere, a door that opens on a brick wall. When I try to set boundaries with them—one of my first steps toward self-respect—the friendship will blow up in my face. "But you're *family*." As if that were an excuse for abuse. A few years later, Bob will die harboring bitter feelings, and Sheree forbid me from participating in his memorial reading at St. Mark's Church (which I, in turn, will refuse to attend). Sheree who I made sure was included in the Ed event at Beyond Baroque three days ago—evidence of my own letting go. In the gift shop I bought a Mystery House magnet. (I wonder whatever became of it; it would have held little meaning for me by the time Ira and I broke up.) Close to San Francisco, I spot, off the freeway, the Flintstones House. "I was just reading about it on my iPhone. Neighbors are complaining that it's an eyesore. Look, there are the dinosaurs!" The city finally in view, Amy says that next week she will be flying back to the Bay Area for a memorial for her poet-friend Tom Clark, who was hit by a car on a street in Berkeley.

The following day, before the reading, I meet Dodie (at her request) for coffee at Caffe Trieste. Considering her loss, she's holding up remarkably well. One of her sisters-in-law, she tells me, made the Victorian wedding cake (when I tell her I was thinking about it on the drive up). At City Lights, she reads the Ed poems Kevin was meant to read. A large group dinner at a Japanese restaurant down the street from the bookstore. Then walking through Chinatown with Amy, Randall Mann, D.A. Powell, and Sam Sax. Grant Avenue deserted at this hour of night. Just us. Some wooden crates and garbage bags on the curbs. And, strung above the street, row after row of pink lanterns, lit, tasseled, as far as you can see. I talk for a moment with Sam, who I just met after the reading. Mention Holly and Kevin. How each of the Ed events seemed haunted by death. "Are you OK?" he asks. "Yes." I take a picture of the four of them, four poets passing through time, and post it on Instagram. Then a little video of the pink lanterns, swaying slightly, and a crossing signal, counting the seconds down.

MY MOTHER'S LOVE LETTERS

Over the greatness of such space
Steps must be gentle.
—Hart Crane

When my mother died in 1996, my sister handed me a bundle of letters wrapped in a white ribbon. I knew these to be my parents' love letters, which my mother had always kept in the drawer of her bedside table. "Dad's just going to throw them out," Jenny said. "You should take them." I brought them home (from California to New York), but couldn't bear to read them. Still grieving, I was afraid they would be too intimate, that they would only bring more pain. And that they might tell me things about my parents I didn't care to know. In 2000, when I sold my papers to Fales Library at NYU, I included the bundle of letters, still unread, still wrapped in the white ribbon. Maybe someone in the future might be interested in these, I thought, but I'll never be able to read them. Fourteen years later, however, when I was conducting research at Fales (on Ed Smith, whose papers are also archived there), I asked to see the bundle of letters. I felt differently by then, thought that I *might* be able to look at them someday. I untied the white ribbon and took pictures of the letters and envelopes, but did not examine them closely. These pictures sat in a folder on the desktop of my computer for another five years, till the fall of 2019, when I read and transcribed them for the purpose of writing this. I'd always thought that the bundle included letters by both of my parents, but discovered there were only four letters from my mother to my father. (This didn't register when I photographed them at Fales.) The letters are written in blue ink in what I've elsewhere called my mother's "large, slightly loopy handwriting slanting towards the right," on stationery with scalloped, gold-tinged edges. They tell the following story:

On Friday, August 4, 1950, Joyce, aged nineteen, takes an all-night train from Albuquerque, New Mexico, to Pasadena, California. She travels with her half-brother Jack, who's eleven. Jack meets a boy his age on the train and is too wound up to sleep. He finally dozes off after eleven o'clock. But is up again at 4:30 a.m. Joyce doesn't get much sleep. They arrive in Pasadena Saturday morning at 7:00 and are met by a man from the paint factory (a friend of her stepfather), who loans Joyce his Lincoln. They stay with their grandmother at 555 West Montecito Avenue in Sierra Madre. Joyce has been dating Rupert, an engineering student at the University of New Mexico. At 1:15 that afternoon, as her grandmother takes a nap, Joyce writes him a letter. (She will write three more over the next three days.) She is in the living room, playing records as she writes. The Lincoln, she tells him, "drives like a dream." So far she hasn't stalled. She asks if he's heard the song "Count Every Star"; it fits the spot they're in. "I could have cried when I said good-by to you at the station," she says. "I can't tell you enough how much I love you & wish I was in your arms." When her grandmother wakes up, she takes her shopping in Pasadena.

Her grandmother buys a rose sweater; Joyce buys a dark green sweater and "some unmentionables." The sweater will go nicely with her new skirts. She also buys their return tickets—she can't wait to get back to Albuquerque. Back to Rupert. Not much happens during her week-long stay; she worries that her letters are boring. Sunday morning, she accompanies her grandmother to church. ("A regular saint, don't you think?") She visits two girlfriends, Mabel and Marjie. Mabel has gotten married against her parents' wishes, to an eighteen-year-old named Tom, who "doesn't have a good job." But they have a cute apartment, Tom is good-looking and nice. "They seemed very much in love so I pray it works out." Marjie tells Joyce that three-fourths of the girls in their high school class are now married. "We decided we would be old maids forever if we couldn't do better than marrying a ditch digger." On Monday, her stepfather calls to tell her he's about to sign papers to buy a house on Hermosa Drive in Albuquerque. Joyce is happy about this, and knows Rupert will be, too. She starts getting things packed and ready to be shipped as soon as they move into the house. Her stepfather tells her that Rupert helped him out at his store—unpacking boxes of paint. "I hope you aren't working too hard." The next day, Tuesday, she receives a card from Rupert. "You have no idea how happy I was. I bet I've read it over 20 times." She is glad to hear that Rupert is as lonely as she is. "I don't feel so bad." On Wednesday they have plans to go the cemetery where Joyce's mother and grandfather are buried. Eighty miles round trip, in the borrowed Lincoln. "Kind of dread it as it's always so sad, but no telling when I'll be back this way." She wonders if Rupert has seen the movie *Rocketship X-M*. "Bet it was good." A "fellow" asks her out on a date, but she refuses; she only has eyes for Rupert. "Will be dreaming & thinking of you every minute until I'm in your arms again."

My mother's love letters are not boring—at least not to me. They bring her alive for a moment. A teenager listening to pop songs, shopping for a new sweater, gossiping with high school friends. And missing her boy-friend. She will attend UNM (majoring in Home Ec), but drop out after one semester—her stepfather needed help at the paint store. She and Rupert will get married in four months, on December 7, the ninth anniversary of the attack on Pearl Harbor. My brother will be born nine months later. (It was 1950; they waited.) Then I will be born in 1953, after they move to Los Angeles, where my father will start working for Lock-heed. Hard to believe I was so afraid to read these letters. Rather than un-comfortably intimate, they are simply sweet. "I'll be so glad when I see you again. I'll make you kiss me a million times." I wondered why my father's card, which she was so happy to receive, was not with her letters. My mother was so sentimental; she saved everything. I wouldn't be sur-prised if the white ribbon wrapped around the letters was from one of their wedding presents. I looked up the song she mentions, "Count Every Star." A 1950 hit by Ray Anthony and His Orchestra. Listened to it on YouTube. A lovesick crooning number. The lyrics do mirror my mother's predicament: "Heaven knows I miss you." And looked up *Rocketship X-M*. Released in May 1950, it was, according to Wikipedia, the first outer space adventure of the post-World War II era. Starring Lloyd Bridges, it tells the story of an expedition to the Moon (hence "X-M") that goes awry; the crew ends up on Mars instead. I watched it on YouTube: pure 1950s sci-fi cheesiness. Not to mention sexism. Bridges refers to the female astronaut, Osa Massen, as "the weaker sex." My mother's world. Massen: "I suppose you think that women should only cook and sew and bear children." Bridges: "Isn't that enough." It would take nineteen years (twice my mother's age) for real astronauts to reach the Moon—a prospect my young parents could only imagine. I've always taken pride that they landed on the Moon on July 20, my sixteenth birthday.

AN ATTEMPT AT EXHAUSTING
A NEIGHBORHOOD IN
CHATSWORTH, CALIFORNIA

Comanche Avenue was insulated by four streets: Lassen to the north, Winnetka to the east, Superior to the south, and Oso to the west. From Lassen (going east), you'd turn right on Oso, then take a left at the first street, Labrador, from which you'd make a right, before it ended in a cul-de-sac, onto Comanche. Ours was the third house on the right. The address (9773) stenciled in black spray paint on the curb. The houses all a different pastel shade, like the suburbia scene in *Edward Scissorhands*. The Lyons (peach) lived closest to Labrador. Then the Silvernails (green). They were the third owners of the house; the Boyers were there originally, followed by the Merandes. Then us (yellow). Then the Goodes (white). Before the Goodes, the Nelsons lived next door. Muriel and my mother were friends; I have a black-and-white photograph of them standing in front of the Nelsons' house: my mother caught off guard, smiling nervously, hand at her throat; Muriel laughing self-consciously, face turning away. Muriel gave piano lessons to me (briefly; I learned how to play "Long, Long Ago") and to my best friend Nancy. Nancy remembers Muriel sitting at her upright playing "September Song," and sobbing. The Nelsons belonged to the John Birch Society. They had a son named Brook. But Muriel longed for a daughter. One

Christmas she sewed a whole wardrobe of finely detailed clothes for Nancy's Barbie doll. The Goodes (from Canada) put in a pool; I spent many summer afternoons playing Marco Polo in it. Next to them were the Weilands (orange), then the Creamers (pink), Hilzingers (green), DeMarios (Nancy's family; blue). In 1965, the DeMarios will move to Thousand Oaks and I will be bereft, left to face puberty alone. The Hilzingers will follow them there. They were the only family on the block, other than us, who had a bomb shelter in their backyard. Next to the De-Marios were the Holmes (Vera and Bud, a motorcycle cop), then the Weeds (Edna and Larry), then the house where a girl named Debbie lived, then, on the corner of Superior, a mystery house. We never knew anything about the people who lived there.

Three cul-de-sacs branched off of Comanche to the east: Kinzie, Marilla, and Needles. Our house faced Kinzie. The Hoyts (white) lived on the corner to the right. Next were the Tates (green). Then the childless couple (yellow) who worked for the studios; his name was Hank. My brother, Ross, did yardwork for them, looked after their house when they went on vacation. They had a swimming pool. And a sign that said, "We don't swim in your toilet, please don't pee in our pool." Then the Mays. Then, at the end of the cul-de-sac, to the right, the house where Nancy's cousin Betsy lived for a while. Across the street from the Mays were the Henzes. They had three daughters. I tried to date one of them (Debbie? Vicki?) when I was twelve. (One of the few times I attempted to pass as straight.) Vicki or Debbie broke up with me right before our family left for two weeks in Miami (to visit relatives). I remember that "Help Me, Rhonda" by The Beach Boys was a hit that summer. The Morans lived on the corner of Comanche and Marilla. Same model as our house, with decorative iron trellis around the front porch. One day their daughter Linda (who years later will marry my brother) showed me her Barbie collection. Opened the black vinyl wardrobe case to such splendor—she owned every outfit, every accessory—it would haunt my imagination forevermore. From behind white curtains, Linda's mother, Priscilla, kept an eye on everything that went on outside. Roland, Linda's father, was a machinist. After he was injured in an accident at work, he spent a lot of time in their garage, drinking. On the corner opposite the Morans were the LeRouxes. I knew Nancy LeRoux (her name is indelible) but don't remember anything about her. The Lindsayes (John and Kathleen) lived next door to the LeRouxes. Mr. Lindsay was a college math teacher. At the end of the cul-de-sac (left side) were the McIntyres. Next to the Morans were the Driscolls. Mr. Driscoll (divorced) smoked a pipe. An older aunt who came to live with them, to take care of the children (Nanette and Dennis), was a great-niece of Abraham Lincoln. She had a lot of family mementos: pictures, letters written by Lincoln himself. The LeContes, who lived on the corner of Needles and Comanche, were cousins of the Morans. They were from Quebec.

If you turned left on Superior, you'd hit Winnetka. Right, below Plummer: the Winnetka Drive-In. Left, Winnetka ended at Lassen. Across Lassen: a line of eucalyptus trees. I loved everything about those trees:

the pungent odor; the long, slender gray-green leaves; the bark like peeling wallpaper; the tops of acorns that looked like pointed caps fairies had left behind. There was a rope dangling from one branch, with a loop at the end, that you could fit your foot in, and swing back and forth. Running parallel to Winnetka: the concrete waterway, which we called "the wash," closed off by a chain-link fence. There was a gap near Lassen wide enough to slide under. One summer, I went with my brother and his friends and explored the drain tunnel that ran beneath Lassen. We lit rolled-up newspapers and used them as torches. On the other side of Winnetka, beyond the wash: the next housing tract. It was still an orange grove when we moved to Chatsworth in 1958. As it was being built, we'd search through the house frames (all sawdust and concrete and skeletal stairs) for the silver slugs from electrical outlets, and pretend we were pocketing real coins.

If you turned right on Superior, past the mystery house on the corner, you'd come upon, after a slight curve, Superior Street Elementary School, which I attended from grades one to six. The playground (which extended to Oso Avenue) protected by a tall chain-link fence. Scattered about the asphalt: baseball diamond, volleyball net, two wooden walls to bounce balls against (that had what looked like doors painted on them, their purpose always unclear), tetherball poles, jungle gym, rings, and, near the kindergarten classrooms, a large sandbox. Must I speak (once again) of the indignities of the playground, how I tried to avoid the aggression of ball-throwing boys by playing hopscotch, jacks, and Chinese jump rope with the girls. Or later, spending lunch hours in the library, reading the blue-bound biographies of famous Americans: Ben Franklin, Betsy Ross, Clara Barton, Daniel Boone, Dolly Madison, George Washington, Pocahontas, Thomas Jefferson. (I was most intrigued by the women.) Or the *Little House* series by Laura Ingalls Wilder. Her whole childhood captured in eight matching volumes. The titles alone were beautiful: *On the Banks of Plum Creek, By the Shores of Silver Lake, These Happy Golden Years.* Years of art projects: cutting an egg carton in half and painting it green, then adding eyes and two pipe cleaner antennas, and voila, a caterpillar. Or placing bits of tissue paper and yarn between two pieces of wax paper and ironing them, to produce a colorful "stained glass" collage. Years of current events. Of studying maps of the world (each country a different pastel shade, like our houses). And models of the solar system (each planet a hand-painted styrofoam ball). Years of report cards. (In elementary school they were called "progress reports.") Grades for reading, English, handwriting, spelling, mathematics, geography, history, civics, science, art, music, and physical education. Grades for effort, work habits, and citizenship: "tries to do his best," "follows directions," "works cooperatively with other pupils," "accepts responsibility," "respects authority." Years of fire drills. And in case of a nuclear attack, "drop" drills: In the middle of a lesson, the teacher would call out "Drop!" and we'd all huddle under our desks with our hands clasped over the back of our heads. All of my teachers were women: Mrs. Wiggins, Mrs. Field, Mrs. Kasower, Mrs. Bialosky (first name Kay, kind and patient and encouraging, whom I had for half of the first grade, and all of the third and sixth). Mrs. Morton (first name Milicent), my fifth-grade teacher, was the opposite of Mrs. Bialosky. Cold and strict, she had no use for a sensitive boy. My grades dropped that year, and I gained weight. Her best friend, Mrs. Price (first name Jeanine), was equally intimidating. The two of them dressed like immaculate Barbie dolls: white, short-sleeved blouses; sheath skirts with wide belts; spike heels. They wore their dyed hair (Mrs. Price, red; Mrs. Morton, black) in bouffants, like Elizabeth Taylor or Jacqueline Kennedy. It was rumored that Mrs. Price, originally from the South, was married to a "Negro musician." Mrs. Morton (with Mrs. Price as witness) often took an incorrigible boy in my class (Jimmy) out to the bungalow where textbooks were stored, to thrash him with a yardstick. The only male teacher at the school was Mr. Bartell. His daughter Monica was also in my class. It was from Monica, in tears, that we learned, on November 22, 1963, as we were lining up after lunch, that President Kennedy had been shot. She'd heard it from her father. It's the only time I remember seeing teachers upset. It was as if the world had stopped. We were sent home early.

North along Oso, behind chain-link, the school took up an entire block. First, several rows of bungalow (portable) classrooms, installed to accommodate the growing population. Then the rows of original low-roofed buildings. A covered walkway ran between them. Then the main office where, behind a long, light-wood counter, you'd find the secretary, the nurse, and the principal, Mr. Flynn. All of the buildings were a yellowish beige; the doors and window sills, a blue-gray. The American flag was raised every day, on a pole between the main office and the auditorium, while we said the Pledge of Allegiance. ("Hand over heart, begin...") Around the entrance to the auditorium: a motif of multi-colored, domino-sized tiles (blue, beige, black, and gray). Inside, rows of wooden pull-down seats descended toward a small stage. We met there for assemblies, Christmas pageants, choir and orchestra practice. And stood in line for polio vaccinations (on sugar cubes—no shot). I was asked to leave the choir when it was found out I was faking (too afraid to actually sing). But I successfully played the flute in the school orchestra. (When my parents were told I was artistically gifted, they bought me a flute and paid for lessons.) Behind the auditorium, hidden from the street, was the cafeteria. And under a covered area, several rows of picnic tables (painted that same yellowish beige). These would be covered with lunch boxes (mine was a red barn with animals—cow munching hay, pig, yellow baby chicks—that had a dome top for the thermos) and bag lunches and little milk cartons (in the shape of Monopoly houses) punctured with straws. Years of apples and bananas and peanut butter and jelly sandwiches and baggies of sliced carrots. On days I was lucky enough to buy my lunch (for thirty-five cents), I stared in wonder, as I slid my yellow plastic tray along the metal counter, at the exotic food the cafeteria ladies (in their white smocks and hair-nets) dished into each section: Salisbury steak; creamed corn; a scoop of mashed potatoes with gravy overflowing from a crater on top, like lava from a volcano; and for dessert, little cubes of colored Jell-O with a dab of whipped cream. Monday through Thursday, word would travel about what was being served that day: spaghetti, pizza, franks 'n beans, grilled cheese. On Friday it was always fish sticks. In the morning: the sweet smell of coffee cake being baked. The cement courtyard next to the cafeteria was where the annual Halloween carnival was held. We wore costumes, clutched our red raffle tickets, bobbed for apples, tried to toss bean bags into the eyes, nose, and grin of a big cardboard pumpkin. Orange and black crepe paper streamers were draped all around, and rubber bats dangled from elastic strings. The library was transformed into a haunted house. Behind a hanging sheet, Mrs. Kasower, dressed like a gypsy (turban and shawl), foresaw the future in a crystal ball. I asked, in all earnestness (as if I were in confession), if she could see my father being nicer to my mother. I could tell my question rattled her, and that she wanted to talk with me at length, but there was a line of children waiting behind the sheet. (I will write a short story about this in college.)

Proceeding north on Oso, toward Lassen, you would pass, on the near corner of Labrador, the pink house where Minerva Herzog lived. She was an artist, and therefore somewhat mysterious; her blinds were always drawn. Nancy's mother, Mary, herself a bit of a free spirit, was friends with her. Instead of a lawn, Minerva's front yard was covered with white rocks. An alley ran behind the houses on Lassen Street. In the late sixties, when I would walk to high school, I'd slip into the alley to the left of Oso so I could smoke a cigarette in secret. (I didn't dare smoke on the street for fear one of my mother's friends would drive by and see me, and tattle to my mother.) One morning as I lit a match the entire matchbook burst into flames and all the sulfur went up my nose. It burned terribly, and scarily (I thought I had permanently damaged myself), and took some time to clear, but that didn't deter me from smoking. Throughout high school, smoking cigarettes was all I ever wanted to do. If you turned right on Lassen and walked three long blocks (1.3 miles, it took half an hour), you'd come to Nobel Junior High School, which I attended from grades seven to nine. First you'd pass Winnetka, the wash and the line of eucalyptus trees on the left, and then Corbin Avenue. Left on Corbin: the alley where Antoinette (who sat next to me in the Superior Street orchestra; we were the two flutists) and her friend Martha would stand every day after school making out with two older (high school) boys. Farther up Corbin on the left, at Devonshire (the busiest street in Chatsworth; it led to the 405 freeway): the ranch house that belonged to Lucille Ball and Desi Arnaz. The celebrities no longer lived there, but their presence could still be felt; we used to ride our bikes up to Devonshire and stare past the white picket fence at the swimming pool and the house, by then painted green. Once you passed Corbin, Chatsworth turned into Northridge. It was like walking through an invisible wall, into a bigger and more dangerous world than elementary school. Nobel was just past Tampa, on the north side of Lassen. Rows of classrooms and lockers and outdoor walkways—in shades of tan and orange-brown—and planters with palm trees and yucca plants, and in the center the grass quad where they set up folding chairs for graduation each year. Crossing the quad from class to class, you could look up and see the pale blue Southern California sky.

The less said about junior high the better. Three years of boys pushing other boys around, calling each other "fag" and "faggot" and "homo" and "queer." To avoid detection, I dated (not for long) a homely girl named Debbie Lane. When she broke up with me to date a handsome boy who was good in track, I wondered if he too was harboring a secret. I went on a few dates with the daughter of Edward M. Davis (who will later become chief of the Los Angeles Police Department). He liked me, I supposed, because he sensed I wasn't going to try anything with his daughter. (These were the last times I attempted to pass as straight.) I quit playing the flute because the kids who tried out for orchestra were too aggressive, too competitive. In seventh grade, I had my first Black teacher. For Math. She wore bright red lipstick, and smoked: When she leaned over to help me with a problem, I could smell cigarettes on her breath. One of the twin daughters of Dan Blocker, who played Hoss Cartwright on *Bonanza*, was in one of my classes. Debra or Danna; both were blonde and, like their father, on the chubby side. And, as the children of a TV star, the objects of much furtive attention. (I will think of them in 1972, with compassion, when Blocker dies suddenly at the age of forty-three.) I liked diagramming sentences in English class, and the short stories we read: Shirley Jackson's "The Lottery," Frank R. Stockton's "The Lady, or the Tiger?," Guy de Maupassant's "The Necklace," O. Henry's "The Last Leaf." Oh the shock of discovering that the necklace was only paste! that the leaf was only painted on! And the wonder, when we studied Greek mythology, that those ancient stories were part of our everyday lives: Ajax (cleanser), Pegasus (Mobil gas stations), Trojans (condoms), Hermes' winged foot (Goodyear tires). My greatest success in junior high was Typing. I literally taught myself to type overnight, and was so fast and accurate (120 words per minute with no mistakes) my typing teacher, Mr. Zimmerman, made me his assistant. In July of 1967, in a summer school English course, I asked the teacher if I could do a required book report on *Valley of the Dolls*. I'd just come upon it in the paperback rack at Thrifty Drug Store. She wasn't familiar with the book, said she would look it up. The next day I was met with a stern "Absolutely not!" She recommended that I read *Oliver Twist* instead. I did, and enjoyed it, but was much more interested in the private lives of movie stars. My mother was also aghast when I mentioned *Valley of the Dolls*, the scandalous bestseller full of sex and drugs, and forbade me to read it. I hid a copy under my mattress and read it numerous times. As soon as I finished it I would immediately start reading it again; I wanted to stay lost in that story forever. But return to reality you must. To the fear of being bullied and beat up. To the pain of being among the last to be chosen for teams in P.E. To the humiliation of dodgeball in the gym on rainy days. To the dread of the locker room, of having to undress, of showering with other boys, of getting snapped with a wet towel by one of the bullies. Averting your eyes from the naked jock whose locker is right next to yours, you dress as fast as you can.

And walk home, on Lassen, as fast as you can, eyes to the ground, hoping no one will notice you, pick on you. Past Corbin, Winnetka, the eucalyptus trees. If you kept walking past Oso (instead of going left to Labrador and Comanche), the housing tract would end after half a dozen houses and there, on the left, would be the vacant lot that we called "the field." This lot, for some unknown reason, remained vacant throughout my childhood and adolescence. Children and bicycles had worn a path through the wilderness of dry weeds and mustard plants. Toward the end of the field stood the Congregational church (modern design, with a wide arched doorway and smaller arches all around the base of the building, so it looked like a tent tethered to the ground) where for two weeks one summer, Nancy and I (although I was Catholic) attended Bible School. We sang songs ("Jesus Loves Me," "This Is My Father's World") and crayoned pictures of Jesus and Mary in coloring books (I made their robes Carnation Pink and Turquoise Blue). I loved the illustrations in the children's Bible: Moses floating in his basket among bulrushes; pairs of animals filing into Noah's Ark; Jesus preaching to his disciples, both arms raised toward Heaven. Next to the church, on the corner of Lassen and Mason, was the Shell station where, in high school, I'd buy cigarettes from a machine (packs were a quarter when I started smoking, then later went up to thirty-five cents). Around the corner, next to Shell: the first 7-Eleven in the area. Across Mason: a row of eight or nine stores (today we would call it a "strip mall"). On the north end (closest to Lassen) was Dorose Liquors. This was where we bought candy (there were rows and rows in front of the cash register): M&M's (plain and peanut), Swee-TARTS, Life Savers (my favorite flavor was butterscotch), Tootsie Rolls and Tootsie Pops, twisted red licorice sticks, Milk Duds, Chiclets, Dentyne, Wrigley's Juicy Fruit and Spearmint and Doublemint, cinnamon toothpicks, Almond Joy and Mounds bars, 3 Musketeers, Milky Way,

Starburst, Necco Wafers (the clove ones I spit out), Lemonheads, Boston Baked Beans, candy cigarettes, bubble gum cigars (pink and green), Good & Plenty (better than Good & Fruity), Red Hots, Dots, Sugar Daddy and Sugar Babies, jawbreakers, Jujyfruits, Pez dispensers, candy necklaces, Pixy Stix, Peanut Butter Bars, Bazooka bubble gum (which came with a tiny comic), small wax bottles filled with colorful liquid (you'd bite off the top and suck out the sweet syrup inside), and around Halloween, red wax lips with white vampire fangs. While the other boys on our block bought and traded baseball cards, I collected Batman, the Beatles, *Mars Attacks*, and the Munsters. It was always disappointing to get duplicates (with whom could I trade them?), and the powdery sheet of pink gum that came with each pack was always too brittle to chew. Next to the liquor store: the barber shop where I got haircuts (there was one of those poles outside, with rotating red, white, and blue stripes). Then the Cornet five-and-dime where every summer we bought a new pair of flip-flops. And squirt guns. And paddle balls. And bubble-wands. And back to school supplies: notebooks and pens and pink erasers and yellow Pee-Chee folders and the glue that looked like maple syrup (the slit in the orange rubber tip would get crusty) and plastic pencil cases (I had one with wheels that you'd turn and it would tell you the presidents of the United States and their years in office; it went up to Lyndon B. Johnson). Then BJ's Music Store. Drum sets and trumpets and clarinets; the walls were covered with guitars. You could take lessons from BJ, a tall bald man in his thirties, but I never did. He seemed gruff, would act put out when I'd flip through the box of 45s next to the cash register. BJ's was the closest place to buy records. Ninety-nine cents each; it took forever to save up. Beginning at age ten, I bought all of mine from him: "He's So Fine" by The Chiffons, "Surf City" by Jan and Dean, "It's My Party" by Lesley Gore, "Nothing But Heartaches" by The Supremes. And throughout the sixties, all those singles by The Beach Boys and The Beatles, both groups on Capitol Records, the label with the orange and yellow swirl. The row of stores ended with the neighborhood bar, The Wooden Shoe. The sign on the roof in the shape of a big wooden shoe. (My mother went in there the day President Kennedy was shot—she heard about it in the parking lot—because there would be a TV. She said everyone sitting at the bar was crying.) Farther south on Mason: Safeway market and another row of businesses: laundromat, accountant, Sheila Rozann's Ballet Studio.

On the northwest corner of Lassen and Mason was St. John Eudes Church. The less said about my Catholic upbringing the better. How many feigned stomachaches (which my mother never fell for) before catechism every Saturday morning. How many confessions ("I lied to my mother"; "I thought bad thoughts about my father") and penances (one Our Father, three Hail Marys). How many Sunday mornings not being able to eat breakfast till after Mass. My mother wearing a white lace scarf on her hair-sprayed bouffant, fingering her dead mother's rosary beads. Kneeling to receive Communion, I was sure the priest knew I was an unworthy candidate for salvation. My father never came to church with us, but my mother insisted we attend, at least until we were confirmed. After that we were free to choose for ourselves. I drifted away, but came back, with my friend Vicky, to pray for Robert Kennedy the day he was shot. June 5, 1968. And came back one last time, a year or so later, to confess that I thought I might (though I knew for sure) "be a homosexual." The priest's vehement condemnation sent me out into the bright California sunlight vowing never to return. Soon after I declared myself an Existentialist (a term I learned in an English class when we read Albert Camus' *The Stranger*). A boy named Clark, whom I knew from junior high and high school, lived in one of the houses across from St. John Eudes. I knew him well enough to talk to him, but we weren't friends. (He went along with the others.)

You'd turn left off of Mason at Mayall, the first street north of the church, and walk two short blocks, to get to Chatsworth High School, which I attended from grades ten to twelve. High school was somewhat more civilized than junior high. All the kids trying to look and act sophisticated, taking their cues from the seniors, who were on the verge of becoming adults, entering the real world. The cooler and more aloof the better. Still, some bullies in letter jackets would push you from behind (they knew you wouldn't stand up to them) as you waited in line at the cafeteria to buy one of those big square cinnamon rolls covered with gooey white icing. Naturally the jocks and the cheerleaders were the stars. One year a girl, a perky blonde, campaigned for a slot on the cheerleading team by driving around the school in a firetruck (a friend of her father was a fireman) chanting cheers on a loudspeaker and encouraging everyone to vote for her. (I don't remember whether she won, but I can't believe such desperate theatrics went unrewarded.) I had the misfortune of being assigned Chemistry right after lunch. The teacher, a thin gray-haired woman in a white smock (she reminded me of Miss Hathaway on *The Beverly Hillbillies*), would point at the periodic chart on the wall and I'd try to follow along, comprehend what she was saying, but found it impossible to differentiate between the elements, and wondered what on earth would I ever do with this information. The class was mostly boys, sleepy from starchy cafeteria food, and their straining jeans drove me to distraction. I was lucky to receive a C in that class. I fared much better in Geometry. For me it was easy (and even fun) to figure out the problems. Our teacher, a woman with short dark hair, was allergic to chalk (of all things), had to wear gloves and insert the sticks of chalk into a metal holder. Three years of French, at which I was competent. Fluent enough to read and understand *The Little Prince*. (Some basic French sentences will stay with me forever. *Marie est malade. Je vais aller à la bibliothèque. Le livre est sur la table.* But after graduating, I will never make use of the language and eventually forget all I had learned.) For English classes I read Harper Lee's *To Kill a Mockingbird* (picturing Atticus Finch as Gregory Peck, having seen the movie on TV) and *Anne Frank: The Diary of a Young Girl* (the paperback had her picture on the cover and an introduction by Eleanor Roosevelt; I was haunted by the thought of the Nazis bursting into the secret hiding place) and John Hersey's *Hiroshima* (the descriptions of the bomb being dropped made me feel sick) and Helen Keller's *The Story of My Life* (I was shocked when she was accused of plagiarism) and Ray Bradbury's *The Golden Apples of the Sun* (one of the stories, about a man who travels back in time and accidentally steps on a butterfly and as a result everything is different when he returns to the present, freaked me out) and Bel Kaufman's *Up the Down Staircase* (the story of teaching at an inner-city high school told entirely through letters and memos and student papers and anonymous notes put in a suggestion box: "Nerts to you"). For one class we were asked to collect similes from the novels we read; I loved doing that. *Julius Caesar* was the first Shakespeare play I had to read. I struggled through it, and would blame it (and the way it was taught) for my inability to truly *love* Shakespeare. Sixth period (Phys Ed) loomed; I had the whole day to dread it. Football, basketball, handball (with those hard black balls), swimming laps in the endless blue pool, trying to climb the coarse, ceiling-high ropes in the gym. The coaches more like drill sergeants than teachers. I envied the girls who got to play less barbaric sports, such as volleyball, and do push-ups on their knees. (My senior year, boys were given the option of taking badminton. I jumped at the chance. And was good at it— fast reflexes.) Drama class was my saving grace. There, students let down their hair and acted outrageously. Although I was never able to loosen up as much as the others, I was drawn to the uninhibited atmosphere, and felt like I belonged, and made new friends. The teacher, Mr. Carrelli (who will discover actors like Val Kilmer and Mare Winningham and Kevin Spacey), was accepting of our various personalities. I immersed myself in the theater, checked out countless plays from the library: Molière, Ibsen, Ionesco, Lillian Hellman, Arthur Miller, Tennessee Williams. And studied Stanislavsky. Mr. Carrelli kept calling attention to my monotone, which, try as I might, I was unable to shake. One lunch hour, as I sat in the small auditorium watching friends rehearse a one-act play, I had the (barely conscious) cognition that I wanted to be up there on stage, but not as a character; I wanted to be up there as myself. (Poetry will one day make this possible.) I acted in Edward Albee's *The Zoo Story* with my friend Ron (I played the mild-mannered character; Ron, the unhinged one). Mr. Carrelli cast me as Snug (a joiner) in *A Midsummer Night's Dream*, instructed me to play him dumb. And to let the head of my lion's costume (for the play within the play) fall off when Snug takes a bow, and then fumble to pick it up. This got a laugh (which I was proud of). In a summer school children's play we put on in Canoga Park, I played a magic apple tree. I wore a tree costume, and at the end of my outstretched arms (branches) held two magic apples (plastic apples that we'd spray-painted gold) for a princess to pluck. My arms would get sore, as I had to hold them up for the entire performance. In the fall of 1970, Leann Renfrow, one of the older girls in Drama, who owned a car, drove a group of us to see *The Boys in the Band* at a theater in Van Nuys. There was much about the movie I didn't understand, but to see that groups of gay men actually existed (albeit in New York City) and were handsome (albeit fucked up), filled me with hope. Mart Crowley became my hero (almost three decades later I will meet and get to know him); I bought a paperback of the play (which I hid like *Valley of the Dolls*) and read it several times. My friend Doug and I bravely staged a scene from it (I played Donald to his Michael) for class. That December, a few of us convinced Mr. Carrelli to arrange a field trip to the Ahmanson Theatre in downtown Los Angeles to see Crowley's new play, *Remote Asylum*. It was exciting to see William Shatner and Anne Francis (Captain Kirk and Honey West) in person, and I thought the play was great, but the critics panned it and it was declared a flop. I saved and cherished the program: the silhouette profiles of the five main characters, facing each other in a circle, against a lime green background. One night, Ron (who also had a car) took me and Doug to see the movie *Soldier Blue*. We exited the theater in revulsion, stunned by the massacre of American Indians depicted at the end. Sat in Ron's Ford Falcon and tried to make sense of what we'd just seen. The last semester of high school, nine of us were cast in Jean-Claude van Itallie's experimental play *The Serpent*. Me, Ron, Cory, Sue, Robin, Sharon, Stacey, Scott, and Barbara (last name Wiggins, daughter of my elementary school teacher). We met off campus for rap sessions, tried to break down barriers and really get to know each other. At one of these, Cory, who of all of us looked most like a hippie (curly black hair, peasant shirt, gaping holes in the knees of his jeans), said, "Some of my best friends are gay." Thinking I might meet some of his friends, I asked him, privately, about his comment. He admitted he had only said that for effect. To make a point. He didn't have any gay friends. Which left me feeling as stranded as ever. I came out to several of the girls, experienced some relief each time I confessed my secret. In *The Serpent* I played the assassin (to Ron's JFK), Adam (to Barbara's Eve; Stacey, Scott, and Cory were the writhing serpent), and Cain (to Ron's Abel). I'd lay in bed at night and run the whole play through my head.

We performed it at school, and then, not long before graduation, at a high school theater festival in Santa Barbara. At the end we sang "Moonlight Bay" as we walked out through the audience. One of the three judges (all high school drama teachers) cried; another, a woman, denigrated us; the third was indifferent. So we were eliminated. That evening, before our cast party, Cory stopped by my Isla Vista motel room (which I was sharing with Ron) and handed me a joint. Just a couple of hits resulted in one of the scariest nights of my life. Unable to function (or attend the party), I floated above my bed, disembodied, enclosed in darkness. I swore off marijuana after that (I'd been smoking it for about a year). The first time I got drunk, on vodka, I lay on our front lawn and watched the world spin. The one time I took psilocybin, the tree I was lying under started revolving, to a tinkling jewelry box tune, and the sky turned pink. I was offered LSD on more than one occasion, but declined. I instinctively knew that I would have a bad trip.

Half a block north of Mayall on Mason, on the right, was the shopping center that ran all the way to Devonshire. Large rectangular parking lot, the stores lined along the inner half of it like a backwards "L." At the top was Ralphs, my mother's preferred supermarket. When she'd come home, I'd help unload the brown paper bags from the station wagon; they'd cover most of the kitchen floor. (If my father was home, he'd yell about how much she was spending.) I'd fish through the bags for snacks: crackers in the form of daisies and whistles and bugles (which I'd put on each finger and eat one by one) and buttons and bows, bags of Fritos and

Chee-tos and Ruffles and Doritos, Hostess Sno Balls (white or pink) and Twinkies and the chocolate cupcakes with the white squiggles on the icing. Below Ralphs was a small Bank of America. And an H. Salt Fish & Chips, where they served the deep-fried cod and potatoes in a red plastic basket lined with a faux newspaper—to replicate how it's done in England. We either doused the fish and chips with malt vinegar or dipped them in a cup of tartar sauce. My mother liked to go there. In the corner of the "L" was the Chatsworth Cinema. To its left, the bottom of the "L," was Thrifty Drug Store. In front were two kiddie rides: For a quarter you could be, for two or three minutes, a cowboy riding a bucking bronco or an astronaut steering a rocket ship through outer space. In summer, when you walked through Thrifty's automated doors, the air-conditioning hit you like a refrigerator. Immediately to your right was the ice cream stand. Through glass you could see the bins of ice cream in the freezer, in two rows of three, six different flavors, like a palette of watercolors: brown (Chocolate), green (Mint 'N Chip), beige (Butter Pecan), pink (Black Cherry), light brown (Coffee), Orange Sherbet. Cones cost a nickel: a tall cylindrical scoop of Rocky Road (my favorite). To your left, through the metal turnstile, was the makeup counter. The display of Yardley Slickers (lipstick) in "five shimmery, shiny shades": Basic, Sunny, Frosted, Surf (blue lipstick!), and Tan-Tan. The pink-and-orange-striped tubes would drive me wild. They looked like little toys, little curios. As did the small round plastic Glimmerick (eye shadow) cases, with their border of blue and lavender stripes. And the names of the colors: Little Girl Pink, Ruffle Blue, Peach Ribbons, Stop White, Kid Brown, Lacey

Aqua, Dolly Mauve, Organdy Green, Quicksilver, Yellow Frills. The trick was not to linger too long, lest the woman behind the counter become suspicious of this boy's interest. (Little Boy Blue would have been my shade.) Several rows over and back: the toy aisle with the Barbie outfits in their pink-and-white-striped cardboard frames (they looked like paintings), the tantalizing dresses and accessories gleaming beneath cellophane. (Years in the future, from age forty on, I will collect those forbidden outfits to my heart's content.) If upon entering Thrifty's you walked straight ahead, past the cashiers on the left and the liquor section on the right (where cigarettes and Trojans and *Playboys* were sold behind the counter), you'd reach the magazine stand and the rotating rack of paperback books. These were my lifeline to the outside world. Comics were twelve cents apiece. I followed Harvey characters like Casper the Friendly Ghost and Wendy the Good Little Witch and Richie Rich and Little Lotta and Little Audrey and Little Dot and Baby Huey and Spooky the Tuff Little Ghost and the Ghostly Trio (Casper's uncles) and the Witch Sisters (Wendy's aunts). And DC heroes like Superman and Batman and Wonder Woman and Green Lantern and the Atom and Aquaman and Flash. I subscribed to *Lois Lane* and *Justice League of America* and *The Brave and the Bold.* And also bought *Superboy* and *Jimmy Olsen* and *Action* and *Adventure Comics.* And *Classics Illustrated Junior* fairy tales like "Jack and the Beanstalk" and "The Little Mermaid" and "Rumpelstiltskin" and "The Dancing Princesses" and "Thumbelina" and "Snow White and Red Rose." And romance comics like *Heart Throbs* and *Teen Confessions* and *Young Romance.* I bought *MAD* for the movie spoofs ("For the Birds," "The $ound of Money," "Valley of the Dollars," "Rosemia's Boo-Boo") and for "Spy vs. Spy." I bought teen magazines like *16* and *Tiger Beat* for the pictures of The Beatles and Sonny & Cher and Herman's Hermits and my idol Patty Duke (the youngest actress ever to win an Oscar, for playing Helen Keller in *The Miracle Worker*, and star of her own TV show, in which she played identical cousins, which I watched every chance I got). I bought movie magazines to keep up with forthcoming films and the private lives of the stars. For pictures of Jane Fonda in her sexy costumes for *Barbarella*. And Elizabeth Taylor and Mia Farrow taking a bath together in *Secret Ceremony*. And Sharon Tate and Roman Polanski jet-setting from airport to airport, Sharon wearing black boots and fur coat and gigantic sunglasses, a movie script tucked under her arm. And to find out who Ryan O'Neal and Barbara Parkins, the stars of the prime-time soap opera *Peyton Place* (which I wasn't allowed to see—too racy) were dating. Then there were magazines like *True Crime* and *Inside Detective* which, after reading a few articles about co-eds being strangled and housewives being stabbed, I stayed away from. Each time I went into Thrifty's, I would spin the paperback rack to see what new novels had come in. Agatha Christie mysteries (I read many, and especially liked the ones based on nursery rhymes: *A Pocket Full of Rye*, *Hickory Dickory Death*). Harold Robbins potboilers (I read *A Stone for Danny Fisher*, *The Dream Merchants*, and *Never Love a Stranger*). James Bond thrillers (which I never read but was enticed by the colorful covers: *Diamonds Are Forever* was shocking pink; *Casino Royale*, yellow; *Goldfinger*, purple; *The Spy Who Loved Me*, green). A book about the history of the Academy Awards (which I memorized). Novelizations of movies I had seen (*Arrivederci, Baby!*; *Sweet November*). A novel based on the TV show *Bewitched* (which I stole by slipping it between my skateboard and my hip, then felt so guilty I threw it away on the way home). *Reflections in a Golden Eye* and *They Shoot Horses, Don't They?* (because I'd seen the movies). *The Exhibitionist* (supposedly based on Jane Fonda). *The Symbol* (based on Marilyn Monroe). *The Walking Stick* ("Soon to be a Major Motion Picture"—which I never saw). One day I discovered Truman Capote's *Breakfast at Tiffany's* in the rack. From the very first line ("I am always drawn back to places where I have lived . . .") to the last ("I hope Holly has, too"), I loved every word of that book. It, more than any other (except possibly *Valley of the Dolls*), made me want to be a writer when I grew up.

From the moment the Chatsworth Cinema opened, July 29, 1966 (nine days earlier I'd celebrated my thirteenth birthday), I went there as often as I could. Rode my bike (five minutes up Casaba Avenue, left on Mayall, right on Mason) and chained it to a post in front of the theater. Paid for my ticket, which the usher tore in half at the door. Stood in line at the refreshment counter. Bought (if I had enough money) buttered popcorn, a coke, and either Flicks (milk chocolate wafers that came in tubes wrapped in shiny red, blue, gold, or green foil) or a box of Junior Mints. Then settled in one of the cushiony gold fold-down seats. The first movie to play there was *Arabesque*, a thriller starring Sophia Loren and Gregory Peck. Stylish, op art credits. Seductive Henry Mancini theme.

And a scene I will never forget: Sophia Loren, in a frilly pink chiffon dressing gown (designed by Dior), trying on pair after pair of shoes (her nefarious lover has a fetish): heels with feathery pom-pons, silky sling-backs, thigh-high white vinyl boots. Throughout junior high and high school, I saw *Walk, Don't Run* (with Cary Grant in his final film role), *Fantastic Voyage* (a submarine crew—that includes Raquel Welch—is shrunk to microscopic size and injected into the body of a wounded scientist, to remove a blood clot from his brain), *The Fortune Cookie*, *Gambit* (I always liked Shirley MacLaine), *The Dirty Dozen*, *In the Heat of the Night*, *Bonnie and Clyde* (adults complained about the violence, but I found it exhilarating), *Cool Hand Luke* ("What we've got here is failure to communicate"), *The Fox* (I had a crush on Keir Dullea and saw the movie several times in order to rewatch his love scene with Anne Heywood), *The Graduate*, *Berserk!* (with the great Joan Crawford as ringmistress of a circus beset with a series of gruesome murders), *Poor Cow* (British films seemed to leave me at a loss), *Planet of the Apes* and *Will Penny* (both with Charlton Heston, who seemed to be in every other movie that came out), *Romeo and Juliet* (Shakespeare took a back seat to Leonard Whiting's bare ass), *No Way to Treat a Lady* (a black comedy based on the Boston Strangler), *Rosemary's Baby*, *The Thomas Crown Affair* (Faye Dunaway's mini-dresses and wide-brim hats!), *Did You Hear the One About the Traveling Saleslady?* (and other terrible comedies with Phyllis Diller and Bob Hope), *Charly*, *Bullitt* (that chase scene!), *The Lion in Winter* (with the great Katherine Hepburn), *The Prime of Miss Jean Brodie*, *True Grit*, *Last Summer* (the rape scene was especially upsetting), *Me, Natalie* (with Patty Duke, made to look homely), *The Sterile Cuckoo* (with Liza Minnelli, daughter of the great Judy Garland), *Anne of the Thousand Days, Tell Me That You Love Me, Junie Moon* (also with Liza, playing a disfigured woman), *The Grasshopper, The Strawberry Statement* (about student unrest), *Catch-22* (certain images, like the man getting cut in half by an airplane propeller or the guts falling out of the wounded bombardier, were extremely disturbing), *Where's Poppa?* (with elderly Ruth Gordon, whom I admired; I was so happy when she won a much-deserved Oscar for *Rosemary's Baby*), *Love Story* (which I saw with my friend Laureen when she came home from UC Santa Barbara for Christmas break; she drove us to Westwood to see it; boy, did we make fun of the line "Love means never having to say you're sorry"), *Little Big Man, Summer of '42* (the first time I heard The Andrews Sisters), *Red Sky at Morning,* and *The Beguiled* (I was repulsed when Geraldine Page and the other women feed Clint Eastwood poisonous mushrooms). I tried to see *Goodbye, Columbus,* but wasn't allowed in. It was rated R—*persons under 18 must be accompanied by a parent or adult guardian.* When I did manage to get in another time (different cashier), I didn't understand what the fuss was about. It didn't seem that risqué, though I had never heard of a diaphragm before. I only saw *Who's Afraid of Virginia Woolf?* because I went with a friend and her parents when it played at the Winnetka Drive-In. The point of the movie went over my head, so entranced was I by the language: I'd never (despite my father's perpetual outbursts) heard so much swearing. I wanted to learn the truth about drugs and sex from *The Trip* and *Psych-Out* and

Wild in the Streets and *The Detective* and *The Legend of Lylah Clare* and *The Killing of Sister George* and *Candy* and *I Am Curious (Yellow)* and *Midnight Cowboy* and *Bob & Carol & Ted & Alice* and *John and Mary* and *Myra Breckinridge*, but none of them ever came to Chatsworth. (I probably wouldn't have gotten in if they had.)

While I was reading and rereading *Valley of the Dolls* (summer of '67), I learned that it was being made into a movie. This was practically all I could think about. Especially after I read that Patty Duke had been cast as one of the main characters, Neely O'Hara (based on Judy Garland). She appeared on the cover of *Look* magazine with the other two stars, Barbara Parkins and Sharon Tate, lounging on a luxurious white bed with a headboard of tufted pink silk and swirling gold grillwork. I began buying every movie magazine with pictures from the movie, cut them out and taped them in a *Valley of the Dolls* scrapbook: Parkins in a semi-nude love scene, wrapped in the arms of her "dream man," Paul Burke; Tate in a low-cut white beaded gown, blonde hair falling down around her shoulders. I added advertisements and reviews from newspapers, and made little plastic captions with my label maker, affixing them beneath the photos. I put "OSCAR WINNER PATTY DUKE" under a picture of Patty, tears streaming down her face, clutching at a huge jar of red "dolls" (sleeping pills). I was obsessed with the wig scene, where Neely snatches the wig off the head of Broadway star Helen Lawson (played by Susan Hayward) and tries to flush it down a powder room toilet. Couldn't wait to see it come to life. The movie opened at Grauman's Chinese Theatre in December. I begged my mother to take me to see it. She finally gave in and an outing was arranged: me and four housewives driving from the San Fernando Valley to Hollywood in a beige, wood-paneled station wagon to see the "sensational, much talked about" film that was "for mature audiences only." Some of the lines will never leave me: "I am merely traveling incognito"; "They drummed you right out of Hollywood. So you come crawling back to Broadway. Well, Broadway doesn't go for *booze* and *dope*." On Saturday, August 9, 1969, I attended a matinee at the Chatsworth Cinema: *Mackenna's Gold*, a western starring Gregory Peck and Omar Sharif, about a band of outlaws trying a find a hidden canyon full of gold. As I walked out of the cool theater into the heat and sunlight, I noticed a headline in the coin-operated newspaper box next to my chained bicycle: ACTRESS, FOUR OTHERS FOUND SLAIN. And there was Sharon Tate's face, her wide eyes, parted lips, blonde hair. I rushed home in panic. My mother could offer little solace. In the months that followed, I scoured the daily papers for news of the investigation. Late at night, when I'd sneak out our side door to smoke a cigarette, my hands would tremble, and when a car would slowly cruise down Comanche Avenue, I'd crouch behind the bushes in our driveway, and hide from the headlights. In December, when the murderers were apprehended (most of them girls not much older than I), it was revealed that the Manson family had lived at Spahn Movie Ranch in Chatsworth— just four and a half miles from our neighborhood. Kids began telling stories of having bought drugs from Manson members—possibly even the murderers themselves—at the north end of Chatsworth High, across the street from the baseball field, before and after school. Two years earlier, I'd undoubtedly sat with some of those kids, on a Friday or Saturday night, at the Chatsworth Cinema. A theater packed with overactive teenagers. Munching popcorn or tearing open bags of candy. Illicit cigarette smoke wafting in the projector beam above our heads. Red exit signs aglow on either side of the screen. Loud chatter during coming attractions. The crowd settling down as the credits of the main feature, *Wait Until Dark*, began. A young woman, Samantha Jones (who resembles Sharon Tate—black boots, fur coat, shoulder-length blonde hair—only a harder face), smuggles a doll filled with heroin into the United States. At JFK Airport, she gives the doll to a fellow passenger, Efrem Zimbalist Jr., for safekeeping. Through the rest of the movie, three criminals (led by a sadistic Alan Arkin, who has murdered Jones) torment Zimbalist's wife, a blind Audrey Hepburn, in an attempt to retrieve the doll. In the row in front of me, to the left, a jock in a letter jacket was making out with his cheerleader girlfriend, a blonde named Cindy or Joy or Judy. Her head stretched back, hair falling over the back of the seat; he had his hand down her pants. It was hard not to watch them. It was as if they were emitting a warm light, and the boys and girls in the dark around them, confined in their own bodies, could not help but lean toward it. At the end of the movie, when Arkin leaps out of the darkness at Audrey Hepburn, a girl sitting front and center jumped up out of her seat and screamed.

CODA: "TWINKLY LIGHTS"

When I tell Nancy that I'm writing about our childhood neighborhood, she says, "Are you going to describe the twinkly lights?" I don't know what she means. In the summer, she explains, when children were allowed to go out and play for half an hour after dinner. Tag. Hide-and-seek. Twilight on Comanche Avenue. In the hills directly above us there would be the "twinkly lights." The lights of the Nike Missile Base. "They were magical." I do not remember them. Online, I learn that during the Cold War, Nike Missile Base LA-88 was part of the "Ring of Steel," sixteen Nike sites that protected Los Angeles from Soviet attack from 1958 to 1974. So the "twinkly lights" in the hills above Chatsworth were actually missiles armed with nuclear warheads. And without knowing it, I grew up under their spell.

BOBBY

lived in the only pink house on Comanche Avenue, halfway between Nancy's house and mine. Lived there with his mother Mary, an elementary school teacher, and his stepfather Jim, also a teacher. Mary and Jim had an amateur interest in music. (They'd met through a music group.) Showtunes and standards like "Smile" and "As Time Goes By." Nat King Cole's "Stardust." I went with Nancy once to visit them. Jim played their piano, and Mary sang. Between songs, they refilled their cocktails. When they were finished we asked, "Can we say hello to Bobby?" Nancy and I both had crushes on him. Unspoken, of course; we wouldn't have had the words. We stood in the doorway to Bobby's room. He was fourteen, four years older than us. Handsome. Jet-black hair. He lay on a twin bed, arms behind his head, with an expression that was—what?—cocky? flattered by our interest? the attention? I'm sure Nancy, who was bolder, excitedly asked him questions. While I stood quietly beside her, observing him. In the mid-1960s, Bobby and his parents went to live in England for what seemed an eternity—two years. (Mary and Jim's one-year sabbatical turned into an additional year of teaching abroad.) They rented their house to a German family, the Schenks, who had four children, all of them blond: Kathy, Chrissy, Patty, and Fritz. One summer afternoon I got into a fight—god knows about what—with Chrissy, the oldest, on their front lawn. My fault or not, my mother insisted I be a gentleman and go back and apologize. Chrissy continued to act huffy toward me. It made walking to Nancy's uncomfortable; those blond Schenk kids were always out in front of that pink house. It was a relief when Bobby, Mary, and Jim came back from London. Mary gave Nancy a souvenir: a little plastic doll dressed as a royal guard, the kind that stoically stand in front of Buckingham Palace. (I'd seen one on *I Love Lucy*.) Red jacket and tall black furry hat (with chin strap). In the time Bobby was away, my parents had added onto the back of our house. My brother and I now shared a large upstairs bedroom, in the middle of which my father, for his own recreation, installed a pool table. My brother and his friends would play pool. Or sit in an alcove and play Monopoly or Sorry! or Clue. (Our closet was stacked with board games.) Or that particular summer, strip poker. How or why these secret card games began, I hadn't a clue. But because it was my bedroom (and I suspect so I wouldn't tell), I was invited to join them. The goal was to keep on as many of your clothes as possible. If you lost, the others could command you to stand there naked and do whatever they wanted, like bend over and spread your ass cheeks apart. Or something equally humiliating. Bobby attended one of the games. (He and my brother were friends.) Already in high school, he stepped into our bedroom from another world. And seemed to lose patience with the slow, hand-by-hand removal of each tennis shoe and sock and T-shirt. "You just want to see my dick, don't you," he abruptly announced. Then stood up, unzipped his pants, pulled down his underwear. I remember where I was sitting in relation to him. His penis was big, had black public hair. We all stared in silence, the carpet in front of us strewn with playing cards and assorted pieces of clothing. The games of strip poker stopped when summer ended. Bobby and his musical parents moved away. I was too traumatized by junior high school to notice.

Time goes by—fifty-three years, to be precise. June 2019. I'm staying with Nancy for two nights, at her house in Granada Hills, after my "West Coast tour"—readings in San Francisco and Los Angeles to promote the Ed Smith book I edited. Whenever Nancy and I get together, the past comes alive. We drive eight miles to our childhood neighborhood in Chatsworth, in the northwest corner of the Valley, park on Comanche Avenue, and walk around. Everything is eerily quiet, the street deserted, like a scene from a post-apocalyptic movie. *Where are all the people?* When we were little, it would have been teeming with life: girls roller-skating on sidewalks, boys playing baseball in cul-de-sacs, fathers water-ing lawns and washing cars in driveways, housewives delivering casse-roles to the woman most recently home from the hospital, recovering from giving birth. Houses the same but changed. There is mine, the trees that my father planted now higher than his two-story addition. Nancy's house is still blue, but a grayer shade. Bobby's house no longer pink, but yellow. Standing in front of it, we wonder whatever became of him. Back at Nancy's, we sit at her computer and in no time (we're good amateur detectives) discover the fate of Bobby and his family. Mary died in 2001, age seventy-four. Jim followed in 2013, at the age of eighty-one; he served in the army during the Korean War. There's a picture of their joint head-stone on Find a Grave: above their names and dates, a cross; below, this quote: "Music our eternal love." (I imagine them singing showtunes in the Great Beyond.) "Oh, he's dead," I say, deflated, when we learn that Bobby, too, has passed away. At the age of fifty-four. In Nevada. By fol-lowing links to possible relatives, Nancy locates, first, Bobby's son, Leo (age thirty-nine), and through his information, his mother, Bobby's ex-wife, Susan (age sixty-three). Detective extraordinaire, Nancy is able to ascertain her phone number. I hold my breath while she dials. The number is good: Susan answers; Nancy explains who we are, that we knew Bobby growing up and are curious about what happened to him. I prod Nancy: "Ask her what Bobby ended up doing." "Not much," says Susan. "Does she have pictures of him?" She does, and agrees (since I'm leaving for Chicago the following day) to meet with us that afternoon.

"This is so strange." Nancy and I sit in her car in the parking lot of Bob's Big Boy in Northridge. "Yes," says my intrepid friend, "but we have to know." Susan and Leo are already seated. We slide into either side of the booth. I face Bobby's son; Nancy, his ex. Susan is youthful for her age, petite, with a pixie haircut. Leo is overweight, pasty, nearly bald. "He drove me crazy," says Susan. "Pacing all afternoon. He couldn't wait for three o'clock to get here." Then, to explain his obsessive behavior: "He's Medi-Medi." (On Medicare and Medi-Cal, Nancy will inform me.) The two of them live in a one-bedroom apartment in Woodland Hills, with a patio that looks out on the parking lot of a Denny's. We talk for over an hour. Nancy and I asking questions. Susan and Leo freely answering them, and offering details of their own. "Do you mind if I take notes?" (That evening, Nancy sipping a glass of red wine while I scribble away in my red Moleskine, we will weave the bits and pieces into a cohesive narrative.) When Mary and Jim sold their house on Comanche Avenue, they moved to an adjacent tract less than a mile away. A larger house on Needles Street, with a pool. Bobby attended Chatsworth High School. Played drums in a garage band. Graduated in 1968. Was drafted and sent to Vietnam, where he drove a truck delivering JP-4 (jet fuel), medical supplies, and food. His truck was stolen when he stopped to buy a pack of cigarettes, and he was court-martialed. (This didn't seem like the whole story.) His court martial downgraded to honorable discharge when the truck was recovered. Back home, he worked as a truck driver (all he'd been trained to do) but didn't like it. Then as a roofer for a short time. Fell off a roof and broke his ankle, and never worked again. His friends called him "Broke Bob." Met Susan through one of them, Larry (a.k.a. "Zonker" or "Zonk"), a vagabond artist who would later commit suicide at the age of forty-three. On their first date, Bobby took Susan to see *Jaws*; the movie scared her. Susan had worked as a lifeguard ("I'm a swimmer") and in a casino at Lake Tahoe. The way Bobby proposed: "Why don't we just get married." "Not very romantic," Susan admits. "If Bobby didn't work," I interject, "how did you get by?" "I know the system very well,"

she says proudly, and reports that out of ten lawsuits, she's won eight."
("You could see the knives in her eyes," Nancy will tell me.) She'd recently
sued her landlord: "Twenty-five hundred. It wasn't a big one." When Leo
was in the sixth grade, Bobby and Susan split up. Susan engaged in a cus-
tody battle (one of her lawsuits?) with Mary and Jim (Bobby and Leo had
moved in with them). After the house on Needles Street was damaged
in the 1994 Northridge quake, the four of them relocated to Las Vegas.
Where Leo was happy. And where Mary died. Bobby and Leo continued
to live with Jim. Until Jim moved back East to live with relatives. Leaving
Bobby and Leo on their own. Susan came back in the picture; she and
Bobby reconciled. On their way to get remarried, Bobby, leaning over to
open the passenger door of his car, suffered a massive heart attack. Susan
shows us a photograph of Bobby's open casket; she and Leo standing in
front of it, like forlorn soldiers, holding a folded American flag. I can
barely look at it. They were forced out of the chapel to make room for
the next service, like a quickie Las Vegas wedding. Leo was upset because
they didn't get to finish playing "Amazing Grace," Bobby's favorite song.
(Nancy and I will wonder if this story—of Bobby dying on the way to re-
marry Susan—is apocryphal. A fiction, invented for Leo's benefit, about
his parents' relationship.)

"He was always my man," I hear Susan say to Nancy. She shows off a ring
that Mary had custom made for Bobby: a circle of garnets (his birthstone)
in the shape of a drum, two gold drumsticks across the top. (Was playing

drums in high school the only thing Bobby had passion for? Or was it to please his mother?) Susan has worn the ring since his death. "It's missing a garnet." She puts photographs on the table, between the cups of coffee and plates of food. Susan and Leo are eating full meals; Bob's is their favorite restaurant. I've barely touched my side salad, I'm so busy jotting notes. I take photographs of the photographs with my iPhone. Bobby as a boy with wide smile, freckles, and baseball cap (right out of *Father Knows Best*). Bobby as a teenager holding a spaniel (its name, Skipper, written on the back). Bobby in Vietnam, age twenty-two, at Long Binh army base: mustache and sunglasses, olive green fatigues, holding up a rifle with his right arm. Bobby in the '70s wearing a floppy hippie hat, red shirt open at his chest, jeweled cross on a long chain. Bobby and Susan on their wedding day, about to cut a three-tiered cake (with white roses and swans); Bobby shaggy (full beard and mustache, shoulder-length hair) in tuxedo, Susan looking askance at the camera, knife in hand. Bobby and Leo on Christmas morning, beaming like boys about to tear open presents, Mary and Jim's blond wood baby grand behind them. Susan singles out a black-and-white headshot: Bobby looking downcast, with soulful eyes. "This is the best picture of him. Taken right before he left for Vietnam. He didn't want to go." (None of these Bobbys are recognizable to me. Was I hoping pictures would jog my memory, that I would see the face of Bobby as he lay on his twin bed, arms smugly locked behind his head, as Nancy and I stood in the doorway? Or the face of Bobby as he brazenly lowered his pants during that game of strip poker?

Those faces are destined, I note with disappointment, to remain obscured by time.) I press Leo for more details. "What was Bobby like?" He was dyslexic. He was a Catholic. He was of Irish and Austrian descent. He had PTSD. Was haunted by what he'd seen in Vietnam: "the chewed-up bodies in fields." He loved sci-fi movies from the fifties. And *The Blues Brothers*. And war movies (though the beginning of *Saving Private Ryan*, the landing at Omaha Beach, was difficult for him to watch). He listened to rock 'n' roll from the '50s, the '60s, the '70s. (Like I do.) And jazz. He believed in aliens. Under hypnosis, he experienced a past life regression: saw himself as a World War I German pilot, with twenty-two kills to his name, who crashed and died. "He looked like Tyrone Power," says Leo. "I'm not gay but I can say that he was handsome." "And funny," he adds. "That's what we put on his headstone: 'And he was a funny guy too.'" (I will search Find a Grave, and confirm.) Bobby once gave Leo a tour of our old neighborhood. Showed him their house on Comanche Avenue. "He pointed to a house a few doors down and said, 'My friends lived there. I don't know what happened to them. I never heard from them.'" (Could Bobby have been talking about my brother and me?) His father also showed him The Wooden Shoe, the local bar where Jim would go to get drunk. "Jim was a raging alcoholic. Nice sometimes, but other times mean." Bobby's real father, Robert Sr., also an alcoholic. (Nancy remembers him—he scared her, had a rough face—before he and Mary were divorced. Mary, religious but a pill popper, was obviously attracted to a certain type of man.) Bobby didn't cry for his father until three years after he died, and then he wept. Leo's hands are shaky; his eyes well with tears. The whole time we've talked, a framed photograph of Bobby, in full uniform, has been propped in the center of the table. Which lends the feel of a memorial.

Susan's voice breaks the spell: "He was a drop-out. I was always the breadwinner." Nancy and I make eye contact. I ask the waiter for the check. Hearing this, Susan quickly tells him to bring her a chocolate milkshake.

HARLEN

I've never known much about my mother's father. Only a few things she told me when I was growing up. That he married her mother, Marguerite, against the wishes of his parents. That they lived in Sierra Madre, California. That Marguerite was a supervisor at the telephone company; Harlen, a policeman and member of the fire department. That when Marguerite discovered Harlen had lost their savings in a poker game, she came home and beat him, as he lay asleep in their bed, pretty badly, with her silver hand mirror. Which led to their divorce. That Harlen died three years later, when my mother was six, of a burst appendix. In my possession (after a recent trip to California, to visit my ninety-year-old father): several boxes (which I packed and shipped to myself) of family photographs and slides. Among them: two photo albums from the early 1930s. The black pages in each are beginning to crumble around the edges; they shed whenever they're turned. (I remember looking at these, and similar albums, when I was a child, but their black-and-white world was distant and unreal, and the people in it, though related by blood, mysterious strangers.) The first album, evidently kept by Marguerite, tells, picture by picture, the story of her marriage to Harlen. The day of their wedding. Their honeymoon (in sepia tones) in Yosemite. Posing in front of their home (a five-room cottage with a canopy swing on the porch and a striped awning). Both of them lovingly holding my infant mother. Shots of the happy family before the hand mirror. The narrative ends abruptly (there are many blank pages) when my mother is three. My favorite photo: Marguerite and Harlen, newly married, standing shoulder to shoulder, forcing smiles for the camera. Marguerite (pretty—she was once crowned Queen of the Wisteria Vines—but somehow doomed; she will die of leukemia when my mother is fourteen) wears a sweater over her stylish art deco dress, and white stockings. And gently cups a puppy in her hands. You can see her wristwatch and wedding ring. Harlen: hair parted down the middle, big ears, prominent nose, handsome tie (askew) and three-piece suit. He holds a pipe (as he does in many photographs; in others, he holds a cigar). And is portly. (He looks like a young Alfred Hitchcock, which makes me like him.) They both have dark circles under their eyes. (When I was in California, I posted this photograph on Instagram with the caption "Grandparents I never knew." Eighty-two people liked it.) The second, smaller album, evidently kept by Harlen, contains photographs of him in uniform, and newspaper clippings about his exploits as a police- and fireman. What I gleaned from these faded notices: that when summoned to the scene of an accident—a car driven by one Martin Johnson "had almost literally wrapped itself about a telephone pole"—he found Mr. Johnson "uninjured but for a cut chin." That he once acted as chief of police when his boss was on his honeymoon. That he testified at the trial of a Mrs. Ida J. Brown, who "got even" with her abusive husband by "hurling lye in his face as he slept." Harlen told the court that when he arrived at the residence, Mrs. Brown was lying on her couch crying, "I did it! I did it! Now he'll suffer as he made me suffer!" That he carried Mrs. Louis Karpf, who was unable to walk because of rheumatism, from her burning home. When a twelve-year-old schoolgirl (whose name was, oddly, Marguerite) fell sixty feet to her death while hiking in the San Gabriel Mountains, Harlen organized the search team that retrieved her body from the canyon floor. Two weeks later, when a man prospecting for gold fell twenty feet into the same canyon, Harlen was one of four firemen who used ropes to pull him to safety. In the articles, his name is often misspelled "Harlan." I sense that this might have irritated him.

What else have I learned about my maternal grandfather from the memorabilia in my possession? That he and Marguerite went on a fishing trip in the High Sierras. (There are photographs: Marguerite seated on a rock overlooking a wooded lake; Harlen in jodhpurs and hiking boots, laced to the knees, straddling stones in the middle of a stream.) That he had a friend named Edward who seems to have had health problems—skinny, walked with a cane. That he was born in July (a Moon Child like myself, which makes me like him even more). That he bet on race horses and football games. That he liked to eat and drink. That he looks like he had a sense of humor, and liked to have fun. In my sister Linda's possession: The hand mirror Marguerite used to beat Harlen. My mother kept it on the vanity in her bedroom. Linda texts me pictures of it. Tarnished silver, the back embossed with cherubs and winding roses. The mirror, miraculously, is intact. "It's heavy," she says. "It must have hurt." (Thankfully Marguerite didn't use lye.) There are deep dents on one side. Such blows would have killed Harlen; Marguerite probably struck the headboard. Linda will polish it, pass it on to her kids, who will pass it on to theirs—Harlen's great-great-grandchildren. My other sister, Jennifer, tells me that after Marguerite threw him out, Harlen took up with a woman (a follower of Christian Science, like his family) who had a young son. When he was dying, surrounded by Christian Scientists, Harlen begged to be taken to the hospital. His pleas were refused. "So in essence they murdered him," I say, "in the name of God." He was thirty-four years old.

Also in my possession: every key, apparently, that Ruth, my mother's aunt, Harlen's older sister, ever owned. Strung on a circular steel ball chain—the charm bracelet of a giantess. In the photo albums, there are pictures of Ruth holding my newborn mother. And many of Ruth, who never had children, standing alone. Impeccably dressed and accessorized—hat, gloves, jewelry, purse (with keys in it, no doubt). Ruth survived two husbands, who left her well-off. She liked to travel. Lived into her eighties. At the end, she said to my mother, "Marguerite ruined Harlen's life." I guess she'd waited a lifetime to tell her that. It hurt my mother deeply. Still, Ruth left her a large inheritance. Some of which my mother bequeathed to me and my siblings. I've always felt gratitude to Ruth: With her money, I was able to pay off my graduate school student loan and expand my vintage Barbie collection.

MART CROWLEY

to be first—

the hardest thing of all

—James Krusoe

In one of the books he signed for me, he wrote, "For dear David." So he liked me after all. That was too much to hope for, or take in: that one of my heroes could feel affection for me. And hero he was. He'd had fame, of a magnitude a poet would be a dope to hope for, in the late 1960s, with his play *The Boys in the Band*. The first to make homosexuals visible, multi-dimensional, real. I'd read it, and seen the movie, when I was in high school, never dreaming I would one day meet and get to know him. He was unable, with subsequent plays, to replicate his earlier success. And what was at first proclaimed a breakthrough, was later attacked (due to changing politics) for its negative portrayal of gay men. So there was a sadness about him. Ennui. A frequent impatient sigh (which I mistook for dissatisfaction with me), as if he were only just tolerating being alive. Being a survivor. He'd suffered the loss of close friends: actress Natalie Wood of drowning; Howard Jeffrey, on whom the character of Harold in *The Boys in the Band* was based, of AIDS. When I'd call, he'd be agitated about something on the news. "The usual ugliness," he said. (I stole that for one of my poems.) So glamour was strictly rearview mirror. We met, as I recall, through Lypsinka, that impersonator of bygone glamour. And maintained a friendship long-distance, via the telephone. Me in New York and then Chicago, he in Los Angeles and then New York. I was respectful, careful not to trespass on his celebrity. And he (I can see now) was always kind. I kept (of course) his notes and postcards. He once sent me Celeste Holm's autograph (when he was reading my collaborative epic about *All About Eve*). Once wrote: "I so love our chats in the evenings" (further evidence that he liked me). He asked me to critique the text he was writing for the children's book *Eloise Takes a Bawth*. (I can still hear him mockingly draw out the word *bawth*.) A section I particularly liked was nixed by illustrator Hilary Knight (who lacked camp humor): Eloise seductively reclining on the edge of her overflowing bathtub like Marilyn Monroe atop Niagara Falls in the poster for *Niagara*. He was funniest when his encyclopedic knowledge of the movies collided with his languid wit. Sometimes after our conversations I would jot down things he'd said. "It's clear Achilles is as gay as a Disney cow." (He was watching the animated *Hercules* on TV.) "The more things change the less they change." (Uttered with his signature sigh.) A producer friend, Arnold Stiefel, was his "Sunday partner in boredom." Once when I was in Los Angeles, I drove my rental car to his place on Laurel Avenue. A duplex, as I recall. Spanish style. The gate opened onto a tiled patio with hanging vines and shocking pink bougainvillea. Inside: wood ceiling beams, a sofa with wide black-and-white stripes, ornate wrought-iron staircase rail. But I romanticize. He served sparkling water with slices of lime (we were both sober). And on a Mediterranean ceramic plate: green and black olives, cheese and crackers. Behind the sofa, on a long table: several rows of photographs, in silver frames, of his famous friends: Natalie Wood, Robert Wagner, Dominick Dunne, the original cast of *The Boys in the Band* (most of them dead of AIDS). On a wall in the upstairs hall: a framed costume design (in muted watercolors) from *Boys*: the cowboy, hips cocked in a suggestive stance, thumbs in the pockets of his tight pants. I admired it when I went up to use the bathroom. He took me to dinner at a restaurant in West Hollywood. His body language changed as we walked through the door: *I am someone of importance.* (He had, after all, made entrances with movie stars.) I'd never seen anyone transform themselves like that. It was both impressive and gratuitous. After he moved back to New York (to the same neighborhood where Garbo lived out her later years), we talked one or two times. But then I let the friendship lapse, which, now that he's gone, I regret.

In one of his obits online, I read that, not long before he died, when *The Boys in the Band* won a Tony for best revival, he said, "You have given me peace." Too much to hope for, perhaps, but I'll take it on faith.

MY COMIC BOOK COLLECTION

The few things I still have that were mine as a child. My red-and-white Christmas stocking, quilted vinyl with three jingle bells, and an attached tag that says "To David from Santa" (in my mother's handwriting), kept folded for fifty years in an old May Co. gift box. My copy of *Grimms' Fairy Tales* (Illustrated Junior Library), in which I wrote my name and address on the inside cover (in the sky above the scene of a prince returning to a castle with a slain dragon). And *Indian Stamps*, "a little golden activity book," given to me as a present, age five, when I went into the hospital to have my tonsils removed. Each page has a drawing, text, and two-and-a-half-inch square in which I affixed a colorful stamp: *Papoose, Tepee, Medicine Man, Buffalo, War Bonnet, Calumet.* (I so loved this book, I grew up believing I was part Native American.) And *Flip Flop Face*, a spiral-bound book with interchangeable panels (forehead, eyes and nose, mouth and chin) that you can flip and flop to create (according to the cover) as many as 686 different goofy faces. And my comic book collection. Over two hundred DC comics from the Silver Age, accumulated throughout the sixties—from 1962, when I was nine, on. In two narrow white cardboard storage boxes, with pull-out drawers. Each comic upright, in its own clear plastic sleeve with white backing board. (I organized them thusly, for preservation, about ten years ago.) A collection made from painstakingly saved pennies. And handouts (how I begged) from my mother's coin purse. And loose change stolen (yes, I admit it) from the valet tray on top of my father's bureau. Comics cost twelve cents and had three stories (except for the periodic 80-page "giants," which anthologized eight or nine stories from previous issues; those cost a whole quarter). *Superman, Superboy, Lois Lane* (Superman's Girl Friend), *Jimmy Olsen* (Superman's Pal), *Action Comics* (which featured stories about Supergirl), *Adventure Comics* (which featured the Legion of Super-Heroes), *The Brave and the Bold* (in which two super-heroes teamed up—Batman and Green Arrow, Supergirl and Wonder Woman, Aquaman and the Atom, Batman and Flash—to rid the universe of evil), and *Justice League of America* (each issue had a roll call of super-heroes who banded together to battle assorted villains). I already loved to read, but comics drew me into new, colorful worlds of secret identities and super-powers. Clark Kent, Bruce Wayne and his ward Dick Grayson, Barry Allen—all handsomely living their double lives. Wonder Woman (really Diana Prince) with her golden lasso and bullet-deflecting bracelets. Green Lantern (really Hal Jordan) and his clashes with Star Sapphire (really Carol Ferris): both masked, hovering midair, zapping each other with their magic rings; he in his green costume, she in her pink. I loved the stories about various types of kryptonite—fragments of the destroyed Krypton, Superman's home planet—and the effects they had on him. Green sapped his strength (and could lead to death). Red caused him to behave strangely. Gold temporarily robbed him of his superhuman abilities. While Red-Gold deprived him of his memories. I loved the Fortress of Solitude, where Superman kept trophies and mementoes of his adventures, and, in a bottle, the miniature city of Kandor. (This inspired fantasies of my own personal museum.) I loved how all the women in Superman's life bore the initials L.L.: Lana Lang, his red-headed childhood sweetheart (who occasionally turned into Insect Queen); Lori Lemaris, a mermaid from Atlantis with telepathic powers; Lyla Lerrol, a doomed actress on Krypton (whom Superman falls in love with when he accidentally goes back in time); and of course Lois Lane, reporter for the *Daily Planet* in Metropolis. I loved Lois most of all (since I identified with women), and subscribed to *Lois Lane* (how I came up with $1.60, Lord only knows). Month after month, I eagerly waited for each new issue, which arrived folded (leaving a crease down the center of the comic) in a brown paper wrapper. Lois with her Silver Age pageboy, her pencil-in-hand ambition to get the scoop at any price, her rivalry with Lana Lang, her indefatigable crush on her Super boyfriend, her endless attempts to trick him into revealing his true identity. Some of the panels are faint because I pressed Silly Putty (which came in a red plastic egg) on them to "copy" certain images. A few of the covers began to split along the spine, I read them so many times, so I repaired them with Scotch Tape (now brown and brittle with age). Lois' craving for adventure knew no bounds. She exposed corruption, dressed in disguises, solved crimes. And continually got herself into trouble and had to be rescued by Superman. Mishaps transported her into the past, where, in each era, she encountered a double of her dream man: Leonardo da Vinci in sixteenth-century

Florence, Robin Hood in Sherwood Forest, Achilles in ancient Greece. In "imaginary stories," Lois got to marry the Man of Steel, and even have his children, but these were, by and large, cautionary tales: Lois' humanness made her vulnerable to her husband's enemies, and led to her downfall. She underwent countless transformations: Madame Jekyll, Cinderella, Reptile Girl, Elastic Lass, the Witch of Metropolis, a superwoman, a mermaid, an alien, a ghost. In the end, it was only a dream. Or the result of being knocked out. Or a hallucination brought about by a cloud of pink extraterrestrial dust.

I also had a subscription to *Justice League of America*. There was something about a group of gifted individuals working toward a common goal that appealed to me. (Was it that they were no longer on their own?) One of the first issues I bought was No. 21 (August 1963). The cover shows members of the Justice League (Superman, Batman, Wonder Woman, et al.) holding hands during a seance. Smoke billows from a crystal ball in the center of the table; from it emerges the Justice Society of America, JLA's counterpart on Earth-Two, a duplicate planet that occupies the same space as our own: Doctor Fate, Hourman, Hawkman, Black Canary (whom I liked because she had blonde hair like a movie star, and wore fishnet stockings—and because she was the sole female). The two leagues join forces to fight the Crime Champions of Earth-One (Chronos, Doctor Alchemy, Felix Faust) and Earth-Two (Fiddler, Icicle, Wizard). I remember reading the comic on the bus to summer camp. And being spellbound by it. (It's more worn than most of my comics.) I printed my name with a Magic Marker on the bottom of the first page, to prevent other boys at the camp from stealing it. For several summers in the early sixties, my parents sent me and my older brother to Stanley Ranch in Saugus (about fifteen miles north of the Valley). My name was also written (by my mother) on the labels of the clothes neatly folded in my duffle bag: swimming trunks, pajamas, T-shirts, underwear, tennis shoes, hooded sweatshirt, jeans. My brother and I smuggled in a stash of candy (stuffed in a pillowcase), but after one day outdoors it was infested with ants, so we had to throw it all away. We slept in sleeping bags on cots, near a tree. Under a night sky like I'd never seen—stars thick as an art project doused with glitter. I stayed awake as long as I could, waiting for a shooting star to wish on, imagining a duplicate Earth occupying the same space as ours, reciting the roll call of heroes and villains: Black Canary and Felix Faust, Green Lantern and Star Sapphire, Doctor Fate and Doctor Alchemy.... The first morning, after a breakfast of cold cereal, fruit, and orange juice, there was an assembly where the Camp Director indoctrinated us as "Woodcraft Rangers" (we had to say some sort of pledge). The Considine brothers, both actors, were counselors at the camp; one of them played the eldest son on *My Three Sons*. (You couldn't go very far in Southern California without running into celebrities.) For two weeks I endured the communal outhouse and the dust and the antics of unruly boys (some were known to put "road apples" in sleeping bags). I shied away from activities like horseback riding (I'd once almost fallen off a galloping horse) and archery (I just wasn't any good at it). I did participate in one contest: You had to light a fire by rubbing sticks together and be the first to bring a big tin can of water to a boil. I won a second-place ribbon. (Or did I come in third?) And went on hikes in the hills, where we searched for arrowheads and the holes in rocks where Indians ground acorns. And helped paint rocks (magenta, white, yellow, green—like kryptonite!) for a large-scale mosaic of an Indian design that someone had outlined in the dirt. I wrote postcards to my mother (which she'd pre-addressed). And spent as much time as I could in the Arts and Crafts bungalow. Instead of windows, it had mesh screens. I learned how make lanyards by knotting strands of different-colored plastic lacing. I built a little cabin out of popsicle sticks and glue, then brushed it with shellac. I made "paperweights" by placing small objects (pennies, dice, paperclips, even dead insects) in the sections of an ice cube tray and filling them with resin. The last night at camp, we sat on logs around a fire and sang songs. One of the Considine brothers told ghost stories. Red sparks flew up from the fire and blinked out in the dark. The next day, the bus dropped us off where it had picked us up: in the parking lot of the San Fernando Mission. My mother was waiting for us by our yellow-and-white station wagon, wearing a yellow-orange-and-white-striped shift (with rope belt) and sandals. I gave her the lanyard keychain I'd made for her. In the car, my brother and I excitedly told her about all the things we'd done. Our dirty clothes went into the washing machine as soon as we got home.

In high school, I traded some of my comics with my friend Laureen and her younger brother. Laureen knew how to say the name of Mr.

Mxyzptlk, Superman's impish adversary, backwards—the only way to return him to his own dimension. A couple of years later, when I was packing and purging, preparing to leave home for the first time, I pulled my box of comic books from the back of the closet. My mother, who was standing in the doorway, said, "You should always hold on to those."

BROTHERS FIVE

It is said that my Portuguese great-grandfather, Manuel Sousa Trindade, immigrated to the United States in the 1880s from the village of Cedros on Flores, the westernmost island in the Azores. And that one by one he brought over four of his five younger brothers. (Nothing is known about the brother who stayed behind.) Too poor to buy his way out of the army, Manuel had been forced to spend two years in the Portuguese African colony of Angola. He wanted to spare his siblings this arduous service. Plus, Flores was a rugged island—despite its abundance of flowers. It is said that the wind blows there all the time, that the sea is stingy with its fish, and that the land yields produce stubbornly. (As a poet, I can't help but be proud that my forebear came from an island named "Flowers.") The five brothers settled in California, in the San Joaquin Valley, around the town of Merced. They worked on farms, plowing and planting barley and wheat; drove freight wagons; found jobs in the logging industry. (It is said that one of the brothers eventually became a "sweet potato king.") Manuel married Louise Jacinto, who'd been born in a Mariposa gold mining camp in 1872. They moved to Oakland, had one son, Rupert Manuel, my grandfather (who was kind to me). It is said (I grew up hearing this story) that Louise changed the spelling of their name from "Trindade" to "Trinidad" because she was mad at some relatives and wanted to distinguish herself from them. My father recently told me that the real reason was convenience: "Trinidad" was a common name in the phone book, and people found the Portuguese spelling confusing. (Still, the rift makes for a more interesting anecdote.) Manuel owned a bar, but sickness (did he drink?) compelled him to sell it. He ended up sweeping gutters in Berkeley, until he fell from a truck and could no longer work. My father remembers him as lame and arthritic; he had difficulty climbing stairs. He died in 1946 at the age of eighty-nine. My father showed me a photograph (which I took a picture of) of the five brothers, taken in Merced around 1890. All of them looking very serious. And all of them seriously dressed: sack suits (with only the top button of the jacket buttoned, as was the custom), detachable starched collars and ties, watch chains draped across vests, handkerchiefs in pockets. Their well-worn shoes give them away. Manuel (with mustache) is seated in front, large hands resting on his thighs. Agostino is sitting to his right. Standing behind them: Joseph Maria, Ventura (who will die in a hunting accident; someone wrote an "X" above his head), and Antonio, the youngest, who looks like Rimbaud.

GRACE

The Central Coast of California. May 2019. My sister Jennifer and I are sitting on her bed looking at old family photographs. Digging through the big plastic bin we brought back from her storage unit. Photos of our mother as a little girl. (I recognize the adult in the child's face.) In one, she wears a white dress, white ribbon in her hair, and stands behind her wicker doll carriage. Inside: a Shirley Temple doll (all curls), it being the 1930s. In another, holding a different doll, she stands beside a modest Christmas tree (on a small table) adorned with silver foil garlands and glass bulbs. And is smiling excitedly. No wonder she tried, year after year, to make Christmas special for us—copious presents and decorations, trees loaded with tinsel and colored lights and Shiny Brite ornaments— her hoped-for joy (her name was Joyce) inevitably squashed by my father's temper, his intolerance of anyone else's enthusiasm. We take out photos of Marguerite, my mother's mother, who died young (and who liked to hike in the Angeles National Forest, and play her guitar). Photos (so many) of other relatives. My mother's beloved aunts and uncles: Leo (Marguerite's older brother) and Mary (they lost one of their sons in World War II), Louise (Marguerite's younger sister) and Al (a soft-spoken butcher). Both couples wanted to adopt my mother after Marguerite died, but my mother's stepfather, Larry, wouldn't allow it; he needed her to help raise her half-brother, Jack. If he hadn't, my mother would never have moved to Albuquerque and met my father, and Jenny and I would not be sitting here. Marguerite and her siblings (Leo, Emile, and Aglae— who went by her middle name, Louise) were born in Bristol, Connecticut, to Edson and Marie Smith. (Marie, French-Canadian, had been born in Quebec in 1880; I attended her funeral in 1961, when I was eight.) I examine a color snapshot of our great-grandmother late in her life: Crocheted shawl over her shoulders, she sits in a rocker in her house in Sierra Madre, on one of her oval braided rugs. On the wall behind her: a framed reproduction of Simon Glucklich's 1925 painting *Spring Song*: a blind girl in a green pinafore, sitting on a bench listening to a robin perched in a birch tree. My mother inherited it and it hung, throughout my childhood, in our family room. (I didn't know the name of the painting or artist, or that the girl is blind, until I looked it up, just now, on the Internet.) My mother also inherited her grandmother's braided rugs; Jenny has them in her storage unit. We dig deeper into the bin. Photos of my mother's paternal German grandparents, Arthur and Grace Gerlach. Dignified and well-dressed, and obviously still happy together after fifty years of marriage. Grace with her netted hat and pearls, Arthur with his round glasses and gray mustache and goatee. After he immigrated to the United States (he'd been born on January 1, 1876 in Danzig), Arthur made a name for himself as a photographer. He's best known for his daring images of workmen on steel beams high above the street, as the Manhattan Company Building (now the Trump Building) was being constructed, which appeared in *Life* magazine. He photographed such illustrious figures as Thomas Edison and Charles Proteus Steinmetz, and later, in California, the San Gabriel Mission, the Yosemite Valley (rivers and waterfalls, the imposing Half Dome), and (my favorite) a road lined on either side with eucalyptus trees. He worked for Commonwealth Edison (whose stocks made him rich) in Chicago, where he met Grace (maiden name Franz; she'd been born in Philadelphia in 1879). They were married on her eighteenth birthday. Their four offspring born in Chicago between 1898 and 1903. Arthur Jr. (who became an artist), Ruth (whom we knew; "She was always a lady," says Jenny), Harlen (my mother's father, who died young), and Earle. Like his father, Arthur Jr. had success as a photographer. During the First World War, he was sent aloft in the gondola of an observation balloon to photograph the enemy—his own people, in a sense, as he was of German stock—and was shot at by snipers; later he was a staff photographer in Europe for *Fortune* magazine. (I learned this from an exhibition catalog of his sculptures, paintings, and drawings.) He returned to Chicago and studied at the Art Institute, then at the Accademia di Belli Arti in Florence. He carved intricate figures from wood and bone (his sculpture of the goddess Diana, no more than eighteen inches in height, "was assembled from pieces of bird bone found on the shores of the Mediterranean before World War II"). He lived thirty years on Merritt Island in Florida, where he made art and was appreciated as "a creative, warm man who had a zest for life and the people he met." I met him once, in the early seventies. He and his wife came to our house on Comanche Avenue in Chatsworth. The visit was important to my mother: She was meeting, finally, her long-dead father's older brother. Arthur struck me as eccentric; I don't remember why—something in his demeanor? in the way he was dressed? I'd just started college and told him I wanted to be a writer. And was embarrassed when my mother played up my artistic talent. (Something she could, for a moment, be proud of, but something she was otherwise at a loss how to support.) Arthur must have felt an affinity, because he sent me Robert Graves' historical novels *I, Claudius* and *Claudius the God*. Which he inscribed in pencil. I'm ashamed to say that I never read them. Though I did enjoy the BBC series; over the course of thirteen weeks, I watched each episode at my friend Laureen's house. (My parents didn't subscribe to PBS.) *I, Claudius* aired in 1977, the year before Arthur died. I'm certain he would have watched it, he liked the books so much. His widow, Betty, reached out to Jenny and told her to come to Florida with two empty suitcases and take some of his art. Jenny still regrets not accepting her offer. We did inherit a few of Arthur's pieces from Ruth, including a pair of paintings of the nine Muses—soft, delicate colors; geometric, Cubist-inspired shapes—which had hung above Ruth's couch (and are now wrapped and tucked away in Jenny's storage unit). We never met Earle, Grace's youngest son, and only know that he married a woman named Signe and lived in Pasco, Washington; she died in 1974, he in 1977. Perhaps he was a businessman of some sort? Harlen became a policeman and volunteer fireman in Sierra Madre, where he met Marguerite. One night Edson caught Harlen and his daughter in the backseat of a car, and insisted they be married. Marguerite was given a surprise shower that was written up in the newspaper. It included a mock marriage (the ring bearer carried a ball and chain on a pillow), a treasure hunt in which Marguerite found gifts hidden about the house, and a midnight supper—the table decorated with a parasol of Cecile Brunner roses. *A seven-tier wedding cake was cut and served by Miss Smith.* Grace and Ruth were not among the sixteen women who attended the shower. Nor were they present at the actual ceremony—only Marguerite's parents, and Louise and Al. Early the next morning, the couple left on their honeymoon: Yosemite National Park, Lake Tahoe, San Francisco. The marriage lasted three short years. Harlen was happy, but Marguerite could not accept his excesses, and was not content to be one of the officer's wives in the Ladies Auxiliary; she was too independent for that. Harlen died in 1937, three months after he attended my mother's sixth birthday party, and has lain alone in Sierra Madre Pioneer Cemetery for over eighty years. Marguerite died in 1946, having waited out the war in Oceanside, California. (My mother would tell us stories about food rationing and blackouts.) Arthur Sr. died in 1954, one month before my first birthday. Ruth was married for almost twenty years to Fred Brown, an executive at S&W Foods, happily, judging from the pictures on their annual Christmas cards—all smiles as they carve the turkey together one year, trim the tree the next. In 1956, Fred built a house for Ruth and her mother high in the hills above Laguna Beach. We visited them there in the late fifties and throughout the sixties. I remember the view of the vast Pacific, the misty light. Their garden spilled over with flowers, and had a stone grotto. The house perfectly outfitted—like Ruth herself. Matching sofas and armchairs, objets d'art on tables and shelves, framed Japanese silkscreens, oversized ceramic lamps. Grandma Grace doted on my youngest sister. Her namesake:

Jennifer Grace. (Grace's own middle name was Vernette.) A sweet old lady, her past a mystery, her connection to us abstract. I don't remember anyone talking about Harlen. Or Arthur Sr., for that matter. (Jenny tells me that after he died, Ruth threw out a garageful of her father's glass plate negatives; she didn't think anyone would ever be interested in his photographs.) But then adults were in their own separate world. They might have reminisced out of earshot. Every year, Grace sent me a birthday card with money inside. My mother would pester: "Have you written your thank you yet?" *Dear Grandma Grace, Thank you for the money you sent me for my birthday. I bought a Cross pen with it, which I am using to write this....* Ruth lost Fred in 1963. Her mother died in 1969, at age ninety. The next year, Ruth sold the house on the hill (for $58,000.00, according to public record; today it's worth three million) and retired to Leisure World. Jenny and I have removed all of the photographs. Only a few items are left on the bottom of the bin. In an art deco case: Marguerite's reading glasses. On a string: a vintage roller skate key—my mother's? And a little salmon-colored book. "That's Grandma Grace's birthday book," says Jenny. I flip through it, find, on our birthdays, in our great-grandmother's shaky handwriting, our names. This is the little book she consulted, how she remembered to send me my birthday money each year. I see that she wrote on some of the blank pages at the back of the book. Six or seven entries, in blue fountain pen ink. The highlights of her life, it looks like at a glance. "Did you know this was here?" I ask Jenny. "No, I never noticed." I set it aside to take home with me.

Chicago. July 2020. I've waited over a year to read what Grandma Grace wrote in the back of her birthday book. Why has it taken me so long to get to know my relatives? To want to know them? A lifetime, really; in one week I will be sixty-seven years old. And during a pandemic, no less. Grace and Arthur lived in Chicago for at least twenty-eight years. Harlen, my grandfather, was born here in 1902. How could I live in this city for eighteen years and not know that. I've unearthed (from old documents) three local addresses where they lived; when it is safe (post-pandemic) I will make pilgrimages to them. The Gerlachs survived the 1918 Spanish flu (8,500 Chicagoans didn't), and moved to California in 1925, settling in Sierra Madre. Grace's parents, William and Constance Franz (her mother's maiden name was Sheller) were both born in Germany, as was her Aunt Helen, Constance's sister; Grace appears to have loved them dearly. (All three died in Chicago, in their eighties.) At age fourteen, Grace attended the 1893 Chicago World's Fair ("many times") with her parents. The exhibit which most impressed her was "a very large Redwood tree, in which stood a huge truck." She also seemed taken by the Midway Plaisance, where you could visit Old Vienna, a recreation of an eighteenth-century Austrian village (with restaurants and shops); ride the Ferris wheel; and see entertainers like Little Egypt and Harry Houdini. "They served fried weenies," she writes. "But mother brought a small basket of lunch—potato salad, hard cooked eggs, cookies and coffee." On Columbus Day, at dusk, they watched "the most beautiful fireworks" above replicas of the Niña, the Pinta, and the Santa María. "After that Papa said we better go home. The throngs were coming so fast for the evening. So we left for home on the Illinois Central." Grace lists the books that were important to her. "The greatest is the Bible. Then *Science and Health* by Mary Baker Eddy." (The Gerlachs were Christian Scientists.) She read *The Autocrat of the Breakfast-Table* by Oliver Wendell Holmes. And Thackeray's *Vanity Fair*. And the Greek philosophers. In Chicago she relished "many wonderful" songs ("The Last Rose of Summer," from the opera *Martha*; "My Wild Irish Rose" by Chauncey Olcott), and plays such as *The Count of Monte Cristo* (starring James O'Neill, the actor-father of playwright Eugene) and *Camille* (with the incomparable Sarah Bernhardt). She mentions Chopin's "Polonaise" and Schubert's "Serenade." And hearing Nellie Melba, the renowned Australian soprano, at the Chicago Music Hall. In her estimation, Toscanini was the "finest conductor." Avid opera-goers, Arthur and Grace enjoyed "the beautiful Grand Operas at the Chicago Auditorium." (She means the Auditorium Theatre in the South Loop, across the street from the Columbia College building where—when there's not a pandemic— I teach poetry.) Verdi's *La traviata*. "Violetta and Alfredo." (I can almost hear her sigh.) Puccini's *Tosca. Madama Butterfly* ("We heard this twice"). Mary Garden as Carmen. *The Tales of Hoffmann*. The Metropolitan Opera Company came from New York to Chicago each year. "The magnificent orchestra, the eloquence and grandeur and talent of the wonderful stars and chorus—How we loved them." In July and August, operas were performed in Ravinia Park, in an open-air pavilion. "We heard *La bohème* in the rain—four in our party—Margaret & George and Arthur & I—Fine." (Jenny has Grace's mother-of-pearl opera glasses, the cracked leather case lined in age-tattered red satin.) In 1916, Grace accompanied her husband when he photographed the mansion of Samuel Insull, outside Libertyville, Illinois. (Insull was a business magnate whose 500-million-dollar empire collapsed during the Great Depression; he inspired, in part, the main character of Orson Welles' *Citizen Kane*.) The magnificent 4,300-acre estate. The thoroughbred stables, the bird sanctuaries, the sunken gardens. "It was like a fairy land," she says. "The exquisite Italian dining room opening to the Shees." (A "shee" is a mound or hill in which fairies live.) "The most beautiful paintings of the four seasons and the most beautiful furnishings." I assume these images were among the negatives that Ruth threw out. Ruth who did not get married until she was almost forty-five, in 1945, twenty years after they moved to Los Angeles. How did she spend her days? Shopping for clothes and accessories with Grace? A lot of effort went into keeping up her appearance. Fred Brown was a widower, and sixteen years her senior. Grace records, with pride, that her "dearest" daughter was married at the Community Church in Westwood, that a wedding supper was held at the Beverly Hills Hotel. The affair was written up in the newspaper. The rites performed "before the flower-banked and taper-lighted fireplace in the church parlor." Ruth, who was given away by her father, attired in "a Reseda green wool dressmaker suit with brown accessories. Brown orchids formed her corsage." Brown for the name she was taking in marriage. Ruth's maid of honor, Louise Hoover (whose husband,

Thelner, was a photographer of note), wore "a Chinese red suit with lime green accessories and a corsage of green lady slipper orchids." Grace wore "a suit of R.A.F. blue with dusty pink accents and a corsage of pale pink camellias." Royal Air Force blue, it being wartime. Two years later, Arthur and Grace would commemorate fifty years of marriage. Together they'd seen a lot of operas. And survived a pandemic, and the stock market crash of 1929, and the Depression, and two world wars. The one child they lost (Harlen) had given them their only grandchild (my mother, Joyce). They celebrated their golden anniversary at the Biltmore Bowl in downtown Los Angeles. Their picture and a description of the occasion appeared in several papers. Grace was "gowned in a two-piece dove gray print and wore an orchid corsage." The guests (the Browns, the Hoovers, Earle and Signe, and two other couples) were seated around a long table "marked with a centerpiece of Wedgewood blue Dutch iris and yellow daffodils." Grace cut a large cake "as a climax to the dinner." The highlight of the evening: Arthur led Grace in the "Anniversary Waltz" played by Russ Morgan and his Orchestra. Arthur would live long enough to see two great-grandchildren (my brother and me). Grace would live long enough to see four. And long enough to see the first American astronaut venture into space. On May 5, 1961, she watched on TV—with Ruth and Fred in their home above Laguna Beach—Alan Shepard return to Earth "safe and in good health. Our U.S.A. is very proud." Of more interest to me is the journey the Gerlachs took in 1925 when they moved from Chicago to California—perhaps because I, too, plan to head west, back to Los Angeles, when I retire from teaching. Grace's account—a mini-travelogue—also tells me how my grandfather got to Sierra Madre—Harlen and Ruth accompanied their parents on the trip. On the first of May, the foursome left from the Garfield Hotel. They'd sold most of their furniture, "except important items we wished to keep," which were shipped by Bekins. In their Franklin Sedan: a new tent and camping equipment. (As cultured as they were, the Gerlachs were not above roughing it.) They experienced both rain and sun as they crossed Iowa, and stopped in the city of Boone. In Colorado, they spent a "wonderful week" in Estes Park, then passed through Glenwood Springs. In southwestern Utah, they encountered so much rain and mud, they took refuge at the Dixie Hotel, "where Brigham Young had stayed long ago." The hotel was full, but "having my [Order of the] Eastern Star and Dad's Shriners pins, they let us have their rooms and we were very grateful as all other hotels were filled too." They checked into a motel in Las Vegas, Nevada, enjoyed a dinner of steak, salad, rolls, and pie. Then on to Arizona. "They were picking peaches," notes Grace, "and we bought some." Another motel in Barstow, California. Then their final destination: Riverside, where they "rented a very comfortable house on Walnut St. near the Mission Inn." They lived there for four months, "while touring the rest of beautiful California and visiting friends at Lake Arrowhead." They bought a house on West Montecito Avenue in Sierra Madre, down the street from the Smiths, and lived there for nearly thirty years. Arthur photographed it: a white California bungalow set back from the street, framed between two parkway trees, Mount Wilson visible in the background. (On Google Maps you can see that the house has been modernized. But the parkway trees are still there.)

At the beginning of this pandemic, I realized that the lease on my car, a red VW Jetta, was due to expire in early July. I'd intended to lease another car, but it was safer (who knew, at that point, how long we'd be quarantined) to purchase (remotely) the current one. I haven't owned a car since I left Los Angeles thirty years ago, but thought, when I committed to buying it: *This is the car I'll be driving into retirement.* That being the case, did Grace leave me a roadmap to find my way back?

Grace & Arthur Gerlach

David Trinidad's poetry collections include *Swinging on a Star* (Turtle Point Press, 2017), *Notes on a Past Life* (BlazeVOX [books], 2016), *Peyton Place: A Haiku Soap Opera* (Turtle Point, 2013), and *Dear Prudence: New and Selected Poems* (Turtle Point, 2011). He is also the editor of *A Fast Life: The Collected Poems of Tim Dlugos* (Nightboat Books, 2011) and *Punk Rock Is Cool for the End of the World: Poems and Notebooks of Ed Smith* (Turtle Point, 2019). Originally from Southern California, Trinidad currently lives in Chicago, where he is a Professor of Creative Writing/Poetry at Columbia College.